FIELD GUIDE TO

G000022253

MICROSOFT
WORD 6
FOR WINDOWS

PUBLISHED BY

Microsoft Press
A Division of Microsoft Corporation
One Microsoft Way
Redmond, Washington 98052-6399

Copyright © 1994 by Stephen L. Nelson, Inc.

Library of Congress Cataloging-in-Publication Data
Nelson, Stephen L., 1959-
  Field guide to Microsoft Word 6 for Windows /
  Stephen L. Nelson.
       p.   cm.
  Includes index.
  ISBN 1-55615-577-8
  1. Microsoft Word 6 for Windows. 2. Word Process-
  ing
  I. Title.
Z52.5.M523N46   1994
652.5'536--dc20   93-48488
                                              CIP

Printed and bound in the United States of America

      5 6 7 8 9 QEQE 9 8 7 6

Distributed to the book trade in Canada by Macmillan
of Canada, a division of Canada Publishing Corporation.

A CIP catalogue record for this book is available from
the British Library.

Microsoft Press books are available through
booksellers and distributors worldwide. For further
information about international editions, contact your
local Microsoft Corporation office. Or contact Microsoft
Press International directly at fax (206) 936-7329.

Acquisitions Editor: Lucinda Rowley
Project Editor: Tara Powers-Hausmann
Technical Contact: Mary DeJong

FIELD GUIDE TO

MICROSOFT
WORD 6
FOR WINDOWS

Stephen L. Nelson

The Field Guide to Microsoft Word version 6 is divided into four sections. These sections are designed to help you find the information you need quickly.

1 ENVIRONMENT

Terms and ideas you'll want to know to get the most out of Word. All the basic parts of Word 6 are shown and explained. The emphasis here is on quick answers, but most topics are cross-referenced so you can find out more if you want to.

Diagrams of key windows components, with quick definitions, cross referenced to more complete information.

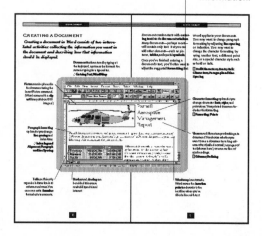

Tipmeister

Watch for me as you use this Field Guide. I'll point out helpful hints and let you know what to watch for.

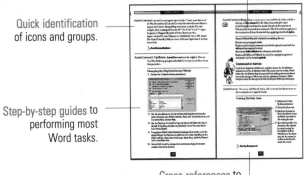

INTRODUCTION

••

In the field and on expedition, you need practical solutions. Fast. This field guide provides just these sorts of lightning quick answers. But take two minutes and read the introduction. It explains how this unusual little book works.

HOW TO USE THIS BOOK

Sometime during grade school, my parents gave me a field guide to North American birds. With its visual approach, its maps, and the numerous illustrations, that guide delivered hours of enjoyment. The book also helped me better understand and more fully enjoy the birds in my neighborhood. As an extra bonus the small book fit neatly in a child's rucksack. But I'm getting off the track.

WHAT IS A FIELD GUIDE?

This book works in the same way as that field guide. It organizes information visually with numerous illustrations. And it does this in a way that helps you more easily and more quickly understand working with Microsoft Word. For new users, the field guide provides a visual path to finding the essential information necessary to start using Word. But the field guide isn't only for beginners. For experienced users, the field guide provides concise, easy-to-find descriptions of Word tasks, terms, and techniques.

WHEN YOU HAVE A QUESTION

Let me explain then how to find the information you need. You'll usually want to flip first to the Environment section. The Environment works like a visual index. You find the picture that shows what you want to do or the thing you have a question about. If you want to write a report, for example, flip to pp. 4-5 since those pages show how you create **documents**—such as reports—in Word.

Next you read the captions that describe the parts of the picture. Say, for example, that you want to include a **table** in the report. The picture on pp. 4-5 includes a caption that describes how to add tables to documents. So you read that caption. When a caption doesn't provide enough information, I've listed, at the end of the caption, related entries in the second section of this book, Word A to Z. You can turn to this section for more information. (These related entries are always flagged with paw prints—visually showing the trail you need to take to get more information.)

Using Word A to Z is straightforward. Word A to Z resembles a dictionary and alphabetically lists more than 200 entries. The entries define terms and describe tasks. (After you've worked with Word a bit, you'll often be able to turn directly to Word A to Z.) You can read the Tables entry, for example, to learn more about creating and using tables and how to place things—such as **formulas**—into tables.

Any time a task or a term from Word A to Z appears, I'll use bold letters for it the first time it appears on a page or in an entry—like I just did for the Formulas entry. This way, if you don't understand the term or want to do a bit of brushing up, you can flip to the defined term to get more information.

WHEN YOU HAVE A PROBLEM

The third section of this book, Troubleshooting, describes problems that new or casual users of Word often encounter. Following each problem description, I list one or more solutions you can employ to fix the problem.

WHEN YOU WONDER ABOUT A COMMAND

Near the end of the book are two additional and very useful resources: the Quick Reference and the Index. The Quick Reference describes each of the menu commands and the buttons on the Standard and Formatting **toolbars**. If you want to know what a specific command or command button does, turn to the Quick Reference. Don't forget about the Index. It cross-references all the terms appearing throughout this book.

CONVENTIONS USED HERE

Rather than use wordy phrases such as, "Activate the File menu and then choose the Print command," I'm just going to say, "Choose the File Print command." No muss. No fuss.

When some technique requires you to click a toolbar button or box, I'm going to tell you to select the tool. (I'll show a picture of the tool in the margin, so you won't have any trouble identifying it.)

ENVIRONMENT

Need to get the lay of the land quickly? Then the Environment is the place to start. It defines the key terms you'll need to know and the core ideas you should understand as you begin exploring Microsoft Word.

THE WORD APPLICATION WINDOW

When you start Microsoft Word, Windows displays the Word application window. In the application window, Word provides an empty, ready-to-use document window.

Menu bar lists the commands you choose to build, print, and save your documents.
❖ **Opening New Documents; Printing; Saving Documents**

Title bar identifies the application—Microsoft Word—and names your document file.
❖ **Documents**

Standard toolbar and Formatting toolbar provide buttons you can click to aid in creating a document and editing its contents.
❖ **Editing Tables; Editing Text; Fonts; Formatting**

Insertion point shows where Word places the next character you type. You can move the insertion point by moving the mouse and clicking.

Selection bar lets you select lines of text by clicking the mouse. (You do this so that you can edit them.)
❖ **Selecting**

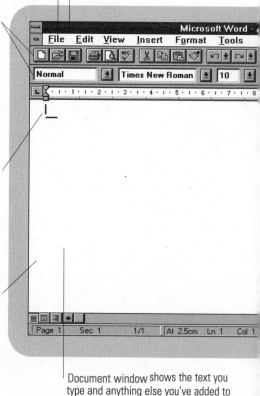

Document window shows the text you type and anything else you've added to your document—such as graphics or **tables**.

Word is, essentially, a document creation tool. That sounds complicated, but you've almost certainly been creating **documents** for years: personal letters, school reports, and business memos.

Simple documents may include only text. But, using Word, you can create complex documents that include text, pictures, and **tables.**

Word also provides tools for preparing elements—**indexes, tables of contents,** and **footnotes**—common to formal or lengthy documents. And Word includes writing and editing tools—such as a **spelling** checker, a **thesaurus** (or synonym-antonym finder), and **grammar checking.**

Getting your feet wet

Learn the basics of Microsoft Windows operating environment before you start learning and working with Microsoft Word. No, you don't need to become an expert, but should know how to choose commands from menus. And you should know how to work with **dialog box** elements: boxes, buttons, and lists. If you don't possess this core knowledge, read the first chapter of the Windows *User's Guide,* "Windows Basics."

Ruler shows your page **margins** and indentions. By dragging the mouse, you can change margins and indentions.
⁘ Indenting and Alignment

Status bar describes your document and background activities of Word—such as automatic document saving and **printing.**
⁘ Saving Documents

CREATING A DOCUMENT

Creating a document in Word consists of two interrelated activities: collecting the information you want in the document and describing how that information should be displayed.

Document text is entered by typing at the keyboard, a process that is much the same as typing on a typewriter.
✿ Entering Text; Word Wrap

Pictures can be placed in the document using the Insert Picture command. (Word comes with a **clip art** library of about 100 images.)

Paragraph formatting options let you change **line spacing** and indentions.
✿ Indenting and Alignment; Paragraph and Line Spacing

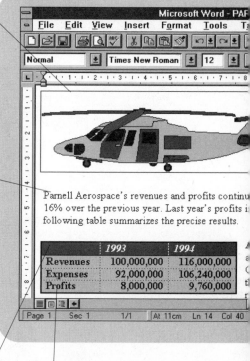

Tables efficiently organize information into columns and rows. You can even write **formulas** that calculate amounts.

Borders and shading can be added to increase readability and visual interest.

Document creation starts with **entering text** into the **document window.** Many documents—perhaps most—will contain only text. But you can add other elements—such as pictures, **tables,** and special **symbols.**

Once you've finished entering a document's text, you'll often want to adjust the suggested **formatting** that Word applies to your documents. You may want to change paragraph formatting by adjusting **line spacing** or indention. You may want to change the character formatting by using another font, a different point size, or a special character style such as **bold** or *italic.*

❖ **Bold Characters; Fonts; Italic Characters; Paragraph and Line Spacing**

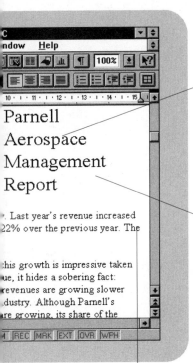

Character formatting options let you change character **fonts, styles,** and point sizes. Your printed document includes this formatting.
❖ **Formatting; Points**

Views are different ways of looking at a document. You choose whether you want to see a document as a long column of text (called normal), as pages of text (shown here), or as an outline of your headings.
❖ **Columns; Outlining**

Word wrap is automatic. Word moves the **insertion point** and words to the next line when you've filled a line with text.

PRINTING DOCUMENTS

Once you've created your document, you're ready to print it using either the File Print command or the Print tool.

Headers go in the document's top margin. You might choose to use a header to name the document file or to date the printed document.
❖ Dates; File Names; Headers and Footers

Colors in a document—such as those in a picture—are converted to shades of gray if your printer prints in black. If your printer is color-capable, of course, your document is printed in color.
❖ Printing

Margins control the amount of white space surrounding document text, **tables,** and graphics. You specify top, bottom, left, and right margins using the File Page Setup command.

Footers go in the document's bottom margin. You can use them to number pages and to provide other document information.
❖ Page Numbers

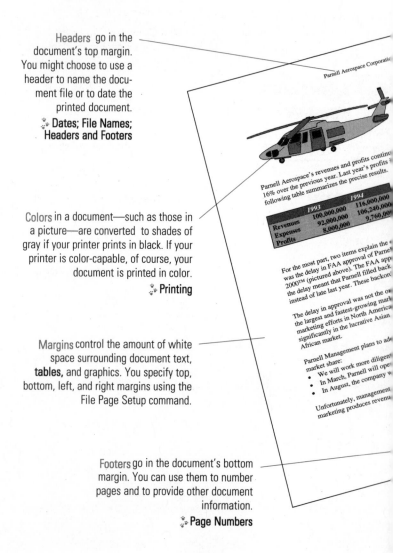

When you print, Word sends a copy of your document to the Windows Print Manager application, which prints your document. (If other documents are in line ahead of your document, you may have to wait for your document to print.)

Word uses the formatting you assigned during document creation when it prints your document. If some element of the formatting you assigned isn't workable—for example, you've chosen a font that your printer can't duplicate—Word attempts to replace your formatting with something close to your specification.

If you want to see how your printed pages will look without actually printing them, you can choose the File Print Preview command. It displays a special document window that shows representations of the document's printed pages.

ace
gement
rt

ear's revenue increased
er the previous year. The

rowth is impressive taken
. hides a sobering fact:
enues are growing slower
stry. Although Parnell's
growing, its share of the
rinking.

nance. By far, the largest factor
uter helicopter, the Parnell Turbo
Turbo 2000™ in December, but
v helicopter early this year--
st $4 million.

er. Another important factor is that
Parnell, however, focuses its
company did not participate
Parnell participate in the fast-growing

y the factors that explain the decreased

and concluding FAA testing.
Singapore and Taipei.
n Cairo and Johannesburg.

e several quarters before this increased

Page 1

Envelopes and Labels

Word makes it easy to print unusual documents too. There's a special command, for example, to print **envelopes** and labels. Word also includes a handy **Mail Merge** feature.

Pagination refers to the process of breaking your document into page-sized chunks. You can allow Word to paginate your document, or you can choose where **page breaks** occur.

TrueType fonts, like those shown here, look the same way on your screen as they appear on the printed page. They're also scalable, so you can easily (and precisely) change character sizes.

❖ Fonts

7

WORD
A TO Z

Maybe it's not a jungle out there. But you'll still want to keep a survival kit close at hand. Word A to Z, which starts on the next page, is just such a survival kit. It lists in alphabetic order the tools, terms, and techniques you'll need to know.

Active Document

The active **document** is the one you can see in the Word **appplication window**. It's also the document upon which selected commands act.

Changing the active document

You can flip-flop between open documents—if you've got more than one open—by choosing one of the numbered menu commands from the Window menu. Each numbered command names an open **document window**.

Active and Inactive Windows

The active **document window** is the one you see in the Word **application window**. Any Word commands you choose affect the document in the active document window.

The active application window—such as the Word application window—is the one that appears in front of any other application windows on your screen. (Cleverly, this is called the foreground. The inactive application windows, if there are inactive applications, appear in the background.)

Activating Application Windows

You can activate a different application window by clicking the window or by choosing the Switch To command from the Control menu.

Activating Document Windows

You can activate a different document window by clicking the window or by choosing the Window menu command that names the window.

Adding Document Pictures

You can easily add pictures to a **document** as long as there's a file storing the picture on your hard disk. Note too that Word comes with about 100 **clip art** pictures stored in the clipart directory.

Inserting Pictures

1 Move the **insertion point** to where the picture should be placed.

2 Choose the Insert Picture command.

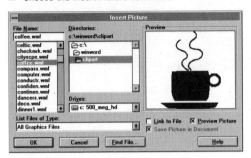

3 Use the List Files of Type drop-down list box to specify which types of picture, or graphic, files you want to see listed. (Picture file types are distinguished by file extensions, so selecting a type actually tells Word to list only those files with the specified extension.)

4 Use the Directories and Drives list boxes to find the picture file.

5 In the Insert Picture dialog box, use the File Name list box to identify the picture file.

6 Mark the Preview Picture check box if you want Word to display the picture in the Preview box.

7 To link the picture to the document file, mark the Link to File check box. (This adds the picture to your document as a linked object, which means that you can easily update the document picture whenever the picture file changes.)

8 If you link the picture, you don't have to save the picture in the document. (This makes the document file smaller—which is good—but also means that you won't be able to see the updated picture until you update the link using the Edit Links command.)

Drawing; Moving Pictures; Resizing Pictures

Copying Pictures

If a picture already exists in a document, you can copy it to a new location. To do this, select the picture, choose Edit Copy, reposition the insertion point, and choose Edit Paste.

Drag-and-Drop; Selecting

Adding Table Cells

You can add cells to a table's rows and its columns. To do this, select the cell where you want to insert the new cell, and then choose the Table Insert Cells command. Word, sensing immediately what you're up to, displays the Insert Cells dialog box. You use it to tell Word how it should expand the **table** to make room for the new cell.

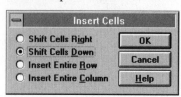

Use the radio buttons to indicate how Word should make room for the new cell or cells: by moving right the cells in the selected row (indicated as Shift Cells Right) or by moving down the cells in the selected column (indicated as Shift Cells Down).

The Insert Entire Row or Insert Entire Column radio buttons insert an entire row or column, so your existing cells maintain the same vertical and horizontal alignment.

Alignment ⁘ Indenting and Alignment

Annotations

Annotations are comments added to a **document**.

Adding Annotations

Position the insertion point following the sentence or the **paragraph** you want to annotate. Then choose the Insert Annotation command. Word opens an annotation pane at the bottom of the **document window**.

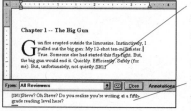

To flag the annotation, Word labels the annotation with the user's initials and a sequential number.

Type your comments into the annotation pane.

Deleting Annotations

To delete an annotation, select its marker and press Del.

Antonyms

An antonym is a word that means the opposite of some other word. Hot and cold are antonyms; so are wet and dry. You may not care about antonyms, but if you do, know that Word's **Thesaurus** provides a quick way to locate them.

❖ **Synonyms**

Application Window

The application window is the rectangle in which an application such as Word displays its menu bar, **toolbars**, and any open **document windows**.

Applying Styles

To apply a **style** to the current selection, activate the Formatting toolbar's Style box and select the style.

Normal

Another way to apply styles

When you use the Format Painter tool, you copy the formatting style.

ASCII Text Files

An ASCII text file is simply a file that uses only ASCII characters. You can import an ASCII text file using the File Open command. Simply enter the **file name** and the extension in the File Name text box.

❖ **Importing Documents**

Sharing data among applications

Word will open, or import, a text file. Many applications—spreadsheets, databases, and accounting programs among others—produce text files. Note, then, that you can share data among applications by moving the data as a text file—and particularly a text file that contains only ASCII characters.

AutoCorrect

AutoCorrect gets my vote for "best new feature" in Word version 6.0. AutoCorrect looks at the words you type and tries to fix spelling errors you make. For example, if you misspell the word "t-h-e" as "t-e-h"—perhaps your fingers fly just a bit too fast over the keys—AutoCorrect fixes your mistake for you. No muss. No fuss. Friends, I kid you not, it doesn't get much better than this.

❖ **AutoCorrect Options**

AutoCorrect Options

AutoCorrect works mighty fine as the Word Setup program installs it, but you can fine-tune its operation.

Changing the Way AutoCorrect Works

1 Choose the Tools AutoCorrect command.

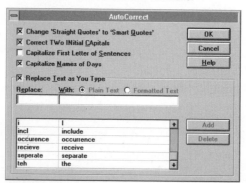

2 Use the checkboxes in the Auto Correct dialog box to select the corrections you want Word to make. If you don't understand one of the corrections, choose Help.

3 Use the Replace Text as You Type option to tell Word whether it should fix spelling mistakes as you make them. You want to do this. You really do.

4 To augment Word's list of commonly misspelled words, enter the misspelling in the Replace text box and the correct spelling in the With text box.

5 Select Add to add the misspelled word/correctly spelled word combination to the list box.

AutoFormatting

If you want, you can tell Word it should format your **document**. To do this, choose the Format AutoFormat command, or select the AutoFormat tool. When you choose this command, Word looks through your document and then formats it by applying standard **styles**.

Here's What Word's AutoFormatting Does:

Deletes extra paragraph marks.

Replaces indenting that was created with the spacebar and with the **tab** key with paragraph indents.

Spruces up **bulleted lists** so that they use real bullets.

Replaces (C), (R), and (TM) with the real, live copyright, registered trademark, and trademark **symbols**.

Command or button

A subtle but important difference exists between the AutoFormat command and the AutoFormat tool. When you use the button, Word makes the AutoFormatting changes without asking you to confirm or review the changes. When you use the command, however, Word lets you review the changes and individually confirm or reject changes.

AutoSave

You can tell Word it should automatically save your documents on a regular basis.

Turning On Auto Save

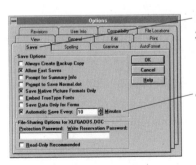

1 Choose the Tools Options command.

2 Select the Save tab.

3 Mark the Automatic Save check box to turn on Word's automatic file-saving feature.

4 Specify how often the document file should be saved using the Every Minutes box. Word saves the document in the same location and using the same file name.

·:· Saving Documents

AutoText

Let's say you find yourself entering something into documents over and over again. Let's say too that you're sick to death of doing so. Or that you find yourself making spelling mistakes more often than not. What can you do? You can set up an AutoText entry.

Adding an AutoText Entry

To do this, first enter the data one last time. Then select it and choose the Edit AutoText command.

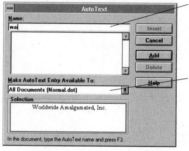

1 Enter a shortcut abbreviation for the long, complicated chunk of text you're tired of entering or mucking up.

2 If you want, limit the documents in which the AutoText entry works.

3 Select Add.

With this AutoText entry, you can enter the phrase, "Worldwide Amalgamated, Inc." simply by typing *wai* and then pressing F3 or selecting the AutoText tool.

Bold Characters

You can **bold** characters by selecting them and then pressing Ctrl+B or clicking the Bold Formatting tool. You can also use the Format Font command.

Changing Fonts

Bookmarks
Bookmarks flag lines in a **document** so that you can quickly move there.

Creating a Bookmark

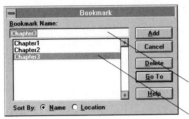

Place the **insertion point** where you want the bookmark. Then choose the Edit Bookmark command.

Create a new bookmark by typing its name.

Quickly jump to a bookmark by selecting it from the list and clicking Go To.

Deleting a Bookmark
Choose the Edit Bookmark command. Then select the bookmark from the list box and click Delete.

Borders
You can add borders to **paragraphs** and **tables**.

Adding borders to paragraphs—**Paragraph Borders**

Adding borders to tables—**Table Borders**

Bulleted Lists
Bulleted lists look like this:

> **Things you need on an African Safari:**
> • **Pith helmet**
> • **Your camera**
> • **Extra film**

In a bulleted list, each paragraph is preceded by a bullet point. The simplest way to add bullets is by selecting the paragraphs and then selecting the Bullet tool.

continues

Bulleted Lists *(continued)*

Creating a Bulleted List

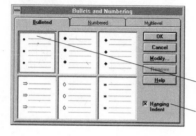

1 Select the paragraphs you want in the list; then choose the Format Bullets and Numbering command.

2 Click on one of the bulleted list examples.

3 Use the Hanging Indent check box to specify whether the entire paragraph or only the first line should be indented.

Adding Bulleted List Entries

To add entries to a bulleted list, place the **insertion point** at the end of an existing entry, press Enter, and type your new bullet point, or entry.

Removing Bulleted List Entries

To remove an entry from a bulleted list, select it and press Del.

❖ Numbered Lists

Bogus bullets

Say you've tried to create your own bulleted list using some cheesy bulleting scheme. Perhaps you're using asterisks, for example. Or, maybe you're using my old favorite—the letter "o" (I used to color the o's in with a black felt pen.) You should know that Word will automatically replace your bogus bullets if you let it. Simply select the list and choose the Format AutoFormat command.

Cells   Cells are the row-column intersections created in **tables.** You can enter text, numbers, and even **formulas** into these cells.

Cells have names. These names combine the table column letter and table row number. The first column is A, the second is B, and so on. The first row is 1, the second is 2, and so on. The leftmost, topmost cell, therefore, is A1.

❖ Creating Tables

Changing Fonts To change the **font** used for the selected text, choose the Format Font command and select the Font tab.

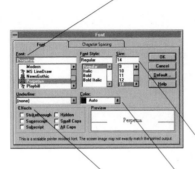

1 Select a font from the Font list box. Word identifies printer fonts with the printer icon and TrueType fonts with the **T** logo.

2 Indicate whether you want regular (roman) characters, **bold** characters, *italic* characters, or ***bold italic*** characters using the Font Style list box.

3 Select a point size from the Size list box. (One point equals 1/72 inch.)

4 Add color using the Color drop-down list box. (Auto [automatic] usually means black.)

5 If appropriate, apply one or more special effects, for example, superscript or subscript, using the Effects check boxes. Shoot, even if it isn't appropriate, go ahead and experiment a bit. You can see the effect in the Preview box.

⁂ Character Spacing

Changing Styles You can change the formatting contained in document styles—although you do have to jump through a couple of hoops. Here are the steps:

1 Choose the Format Style command.

2 Select the style you want to change from the Styles list box.

3 Select the Modify command button.

4 Select the Format command button.

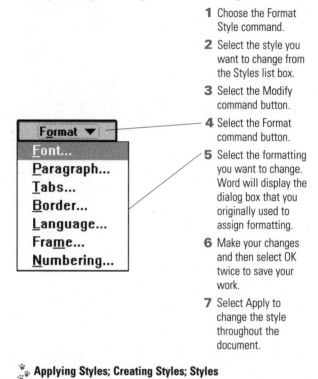

5 Select the formatting you want to change. Word will display the dialog box that you originally used to assign formatting.

6 Make your changes and then select OK twice to save your work.

7 Select Apply to change the style throughout the document.

Applying Styles; Creating Styles; Styles

Characters In Word, characters are the things you type with the keyboard. Symbols that you add with the Insert Symbol command are also considered characters. In some cases—and this is sort of kooky, I admit—Word considers inserted pictures as characters too.

Changing Fonts; Character Spacing

Character Spacing
Word lets you control the way characters are spaced; in typesetting terminology this is called kerning. Most people, just for the record, should not have to worry about this. Word does a very respectable job of spacing characters.

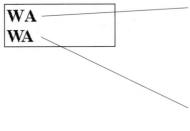

This is the regular way Word spaces characters—without kerning. See the gap between the W and the A? Some people don't like that gap.

This is how these letters look after kerning and condensing the character spacing. The gap between the W and the A is narrower.

Changing Character Spacing
Choose the Format Font command and Character Spacing tab options.

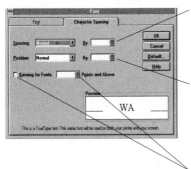

Use the Spacing and By options to tell Word how much space should appear between the selected characters.

Use the Position and By options to tell Word where selected characters should appear in text in relation to the text baseline.

Use the Kerning for Fonts option to adjust spacing between the selected characters. Use the Points and Above option to specify a minimum character size above which fonts will be kerned.

 Changing Fonts

Charts

A chart, or a graph, is a visual depiction of numeric data. You know what I mean, right? Pie charts, for one example. And a line graph for another.

In Word, you can create these pictures-worth-a-thousand-words with the Microsoft Graph application.

An observation

If you've worked with Microsoft Excel's charting feature, you'll find using Microsoft Graph as easy as rolling off a log. Microsoft Graph works almost exactly like Excel's charting feature.

⁂ **Embedding and Linking Existing Objects; Graphs**

Clip Art

Clip art refers to the graphic images that you can paste into documents. Word version 6.0 comes with about 100 clip art images, and these are stored as files in the clipart directory. If you upgraded from a previous version of Word, you probably also have a clipart subdirectory that stores a bunch more clip art files. Many of the graphic images in this little book, by the way, come from the Word version 6.0 clipart directory.

⁂ **Adding Document Pictures**

Clipboard

Ever see the television show "Star Trek"? If you did, you may remember the transporter room. It let the *Starship Enterprise* move Captain Kirk, Mr. Spock, and just about anything else just about anywhere. The Clipboard is the Windows equivalent of the *Enterprise*'s transporter room. With the Clipboard, Windows easily moves just about anything anywhere. In Word, you can use the Clipboard to move chunks of text, tables, and even graphic images to and from different parts of your file. You can also use the Clipboard to move text, tables, and graphic images between Word and other Windows applications such as Microsoft Excel.

To move information around via the Clipboard, you actually use the Edit menu's Cut, Copy, Paste, and Paste Special commands. So you don't have to know all that much about the Clipboard to make good use of it. One thing you should remember about the Clipboard, however, is that it stores what you've copied or cut temporarily. After you copy or cut, the next time you do so, the previous Clipboard contents are replaced. And when you exit Windows, the Clipboard contents are erased.

Object Linking and Embedding

Closing Documents
You close **documents** so that they don't consume memory, so that they don't clutter your screen, and so that they don't just plain annoy you.

Closing a Single Document
To close a single document, either double-click its Control-menu box, or be sure the document is selected and then choose the File Close command.

Closing All Open Documents
To close all the open **document windows** at once, hold down Shift and then choose the File Close All command.

A thoughtful Word
Word won't close a document that you have changed but not yet saved. It will first ask if you want to save your changes. If you say, "Well, yeah, that seems like a good idea," Word saves the document.

Coloring Documents

You can color the selected document background area. This changes the document color on the screen and, if you print the document with a color-capable printer, changes the printed document colors too.

Adding Background Color to a Document

To add background colors to the selected document area, follow these steps:

1 Choose the Format Borders and Shading command.

2 Select the Shading tab.

3 Activate the Background drop-down list box.

4 Click the color you want. Try to be tasteful, OK?

Changing the Shading Color in a Document

To change the foreground (shading) color of the selected document area —which means changing the color of the dots used to shade— you follow these steps:

1 Choose the Format Borders and Shading command.

2 Select the Shading tab.

3 Activate the Foreground drop-down list box.

4 Click the color you want.

Removing Color from a Document

To return the selected document area's color to the default color scheme—the always popular black on white —follow these steps:

1 Choose the Format Borders and Shading command.

2 Select the Shading tab.

3 Activate the Foreground drop-down list box.

4 Click the Auto selection.

5 Activate the Background drop-down list box.

6 Click the Auto selection. Yes, again.

Coloring Text; Formatting

If your audience includes men

As many as 1 in 12 males has what's commonly described as "color blindness." If your audience includes males, therefore, consider avoiding the red-green color combinations that many males have trouble differentiating.

Coloring Text

You can color the characters in the current **document** selection. As you might guess, changing character color shows up on your screen if you've got a color monitor. It shows up in your printed documents too as long as you've got a color-capable printer.

Adding Color to Characters

To change the color of the characters in the current document selection, follow these steps:

1 Choose the Format Font command.
2 Select the Font tab.
3 Activate the Color drop-down list box.
4 Click the color you want.

Removing Color from Characters

To change the color of the characters in the current document selection to basic black, follow these steps:

1 Choose the Format Font command.
2 Select the Font tab.
3 Activate the Color drop-down list box.
4 Click the Auto color button.

Colorful characters

As you start working with color, you should know that there's a reason publishers such as Microsoft Press use black ink on white paper. Black on white provides for maximum contrast and, therefore, maximum legibility. Any time you decrease the contrast, you reduce legibility.

Column Breaks You can choose where Word breaks, or ends, one column of text and starts a new column. (Word starts the new column either adjacent to the old column or on a new page.) To do this, place the **insertion point** where you want the break. Then choose the Insert Break command and mark the Column Break radio button.

Word draws a dotted line and writes the words "Column Break" on the line to show where column breaks occur. On a one-column page, a column break is equivalent to a page break.

 Columns

Columns Some documents use more than one column of text on a page. Newspapers do this, for example. So do many newsletters and magazines.

You can specify that Word print several columns of text on a page by selecting the text, choosing the Columns tool, and then indicating how many columns you want on a page.

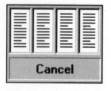

Select the first column in the list, and Word uses 1 column. Select the second column, and Word uses 2 columns. I bet you can guess how many columns Word uses if you select the third or the fourth column.

Column Breaks

Combining Files
You can insert a file—including a Word document—into the active document. Doing so allows you to combine documents.

Inserting a File

To add a file to a document, follow these steps:

1 Position the **insertion point** at the document location where the file should be inserted.

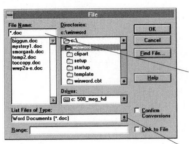

2 Choose the Insert File command. Word displays the File dialog box.

3 Use the File Name list box to identify the file.

4 Use the Drives and Directories list boxes to find the text file.

5 Use the List Files of Type drop-down list box to specify which types of files you want to see listed.

6 Select OK.

🐾 **Opening Documents; Saving Documents**

Control-menu Commands

Control-menu commands appear, not surprisingly, on the Control menus of **application windows, document windows,** and **dialog boxes**. To activate the Control menu of a window or a dialog box, you click the Control-menu box. (It's the little hyphen-in-a-box in the upper left corner of the window or the dialog box.) Control-menu commands let you manipulate the window or the dialog box in the following ways.

Restore

Undoes the last minimize or maximize command. Handy if you're fooling around with the Control menu and you make a terrible mistake.

Move

Tells Windows you want to move the window or the dialog box. Windows, ever mindful of your feelings, changes the mouse pointer to a 4-headed arrow. Once this happens, use the direction keys to change the screen position of the window or the dialog box.

Size

Tells Windows you want to change the size of the window. When you choose this command, Windows changes the mouse pointer to a four-headed arrow. You change the window size by using the Up and Down direction keys to move the bottom border and by using the Left and Right direction keys to move the right border.

Minimize

Tells Windows in no uncertain terms that it should remove the window from the screen. Windows follows your command, but to remind you of the minimized window, it displays a tiny picture, called an icon. Because you can't see the Control menu of a minimized window, simply click a minimized window icon to display its Control menu.

Maximize

Tells Window that it should make the window or the dialog box as big as it can. If you maximize an application window—such as Word's—Windows makes the application window as big as your screen. In Word, by the way, document windows are maximized so that they fill the application window.

Close

Removes the window or the dialog box from the screen. There's more
to this command than first meets the eye, however. If you close an
application window, you actually close the application and any files
that might be open in that application. If you close a document
window, you close only the document displayed in the document
window. If the document hasn't yet been saved, Word will ask if you
want to do this before it closes the document. If you close a dialog
box, it's the same thing as selecting Cancel.

Switch To

Cool. A power-user tool. This command appears only on the Control
menus of application windows. It tells Windows that you want to see
the Task List manager—presumably so that you can start another
Windows application—or that you want to activate another
application you've previously started.

About the Control menu commands

You won't always see all these commands on a Control menu. Windows displays
only those that make sense in the current situation.

 Closing Documents; Switching Tasks

Copying Formatting
You can copy the formatting you've as-
signed to a **character** or to a **paragraph** using the Format
Painter tool.

 To use the Format Painter tool, select the character or the paragraph with the formatting you want to copy. Select the Format
Painter tool. Then drag the mouse over the characters or paragraphs you want formatted.

Paragraph vs. character formatting

How much of the formatting the Format Painter tool copies
depends on what you select before choosing the tool. If you
select a character or a set of characters, Format Painter copies
only character formatting—such as font styles and point
sizes.If you select a paragraph, Format Painter copies both
character formatting and paragraph formatting.

Copying Tables Can you copy a table? Sure. Here's how:

1 Select the table by clicking a cell and then choosing the Table Select Table command.

2 Choose the Edit Copy command.

3 Place the insertion point at the exact point where the copied table should be placed.

4 Choose the Edit Paste Cells command.

∴ **Creating Tables; Drag-and-Drop**

Copying Text Word lets you copy the text you have in a document. All you need to do is select the text—for example, by clicking or dragging—choose Edit Copy, reposition the **insertion point** to the place you want the text copied, and choose Edit Paste. Word copies the text and any formatting you've assigned.

∴ **Copying Formatting; Copying Tables; Copying Text Without Formatting; Drag-and-Drop; Selecting**

Copying Text Without Formatting This is sort of a trick. You might even want to try it out on a friend.

1 Select the text.

2 Choose the Edit Copy command.

3 Position the insertion point where you want to copy the unformatted text.

4 Choose the Edit Paste Special command. Word displays the Paste Special dialog box.

5 Select the Unformatted Text option, and then choose OK.

∴ **Moving Pictures; Resizing Pictures**

Creating Styles You've got several ways to create styles, but I'm only going to describe the easiest. Here's what you do. First format a chunk of your document—probably a paragraph or a group of paragraphs—so that it includes all the font, paragraph, tab, border, frame, language, and numbering formats you want to combine in a style. Then select the Style tool on the Formatting toolbar and type the name you want to give the style. Voila. You've just created a style.

❖ Applying Styles; Changing Styles; Formatting; Styles

Creating Tables To add a **table** to a **document**, place the **insertion point** where the table should go. Then choose the Table Insert Table command.

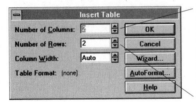

Tell Word how many columns you want. Don't worry about being too precise. It's easy to add columns (and rows) later on.

Tell Word how many rows you want and then select OK. Word inserts the table.

10/6/95	Arrive Kinshasa
10/7/95-10/11/95	On Congo River
10/11/95-10/24/95	Overland to Nairobi

To fill in the table, simply click the cells, or input blanks, and type whatever you want. I added some borders to this table to make it prettier. I also entered some data into the table cells.

❖ Adding Table Cells; Table Borders

A tip for spreadsheet users

You can use Word tables like miniature spreadsheets. For example, you can enter formulas into cells that reference the values in other cells.

Cursor　People sometimes call the **insertion point** a cursor. You can call it that if you want. One of the fun things about being an adult is that you often get to make your own decisions. In this book, I'm going to call the insertion point an insertion point.

Databases　You can insert database records stored in an external database—including a Microsoft Excel list—into a Word **document**. Word places the inserted database records into the rows of a **table**. To insert database records, choose the Insert Database command.

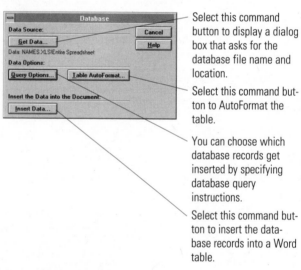

Select this command button to display a dialog box that asks for the database file name and location.

Select this command button to AutoFormat the table.

You can choose which database records get inserted by specifying database query instructions.

Select this command button to insert the database records into a Word table.

❖ **Opening Documents**

Datasheet　A datasheet holds the data you plot in a **graph**. When you select a **table** and then the Insert Chart tool, Word places the table's data into an Microsoft Graph datasheet. It also uses the datasheet's data to draw a chart.

One other thing I'll mention is this: You don't ever have to worry about or work with datasheets. Word will take care of moving table data to a datasheet. It's always those little, thoughtful, extra touches that really count.

Dates   You can enter a field for the current system date at the insertion point by pressing Alt+Shift+D. Word enters the date in MM/DD/YY format. So, if it's October 7, 1994, Word enters 10/7/94. Go ahead. Try it. Neat, don't you think? (By the way, Word gets the date from the system date.)

You can also use the Insert Date and Time command, but mark the Insert as Field check box to make the date a field.

 Times

Updating a date field

To update a date field you've inserted in a document, click it and then press F9.

Deleting

Deleting annotations—	**Annotations**
Deleting files—	**Erasing Documents**
Deleting text—	**Erasing**
Removing table columns and rows—	**Deleting Columns and Rows**
Removing footnotes and endnotes—	**Footnotes and Endnotes**
Removing revision marks—	**Revision Marks**

Deleting Columns and Rows   To delete columns or rows from a table, click on a cell in the column or row you want to delete. Select the column or row using the Table Select Column or Table Select Row command. Then select the Table Delete Rows or Table Delete Columns command.

 Creating Tables

Dialog Box

A dialog box is simply an on-screen form you fill out to tell Word how it should complete some command. Any command name followed by ellipses (...) displays a dialog box.

Documents

A document is what you see in the white area of the Word window. So, it includes the text you type, the pictures you add, and the **tables** you build. You store documents as separate files on your disk.

Document Views

You can look at a document on-screen in several ways using the View Normal, View Outline, View Page Layout, and View Master Document commands.

You can also use the View buttons to flip-flop between the Normal, Page Layout, and Outline views. The View buttons appear at the left end of the horizontal scroll bar.

Normal Document View

 Choose the View Normal command or button to look at a document as a long, uninterrupted column of text, pictures, tables, and whatever else you've added.

Outline Document View

 Choose the View Outline command or button to look at a document as an outline built from your headings.

Page Layout Document View

 Choose the View Page Layout command or button to see how your document would look as printed pages. You can also add **headers and footers** using this view.

Master Document View

Choose the View Master Document command to look at a document as an outline that can name other documents in its headings.

 Outlining

Document Window

The document window is the rectangle Word uses to display your **documents.** If you have more than one document open, the **application window** stacks the documents, one on top of the other. You won't be able to see any but the active document window, however, unless you resize the document window so that it doesn't fill the application window.

✦ Control-menu Commands

Drag-and-Drop

Drag-and-drop is a technique that lets you move and copy pieces of a document with the mouse.

Moving with Drag-and-Drop

To move some piece of a document—such as a line of text, a paragraph, or a picture—select it and then drag it to its new location.

Copying with Drag-and-Drop

To copy some piece of a document—such as a chunk of text or a picture—select it, press Ctrl, and then drag it to its new location.

Drawing

Word comes with a Drawing toolbar. If you're the artistic type, you can add attractive graphic objects to your **documents.** If you're not the artistic type, you can still add graphic objects to your documents—but they may not look all that attractive.

Adding Graphic Objects to a Document

To add a simple, hand-drawn graphic to a document, select the Drawing tool from the Standard toolbar. Word adds the Drawing toolbar at the bottom of the Word application window. Use its buttons to draw, color, and position objects such as lines, rectangles, and ovals.

Drawing Straight Lines

Select the Line tool. Click where you want the line to start; then drag the mouse to where you want the line to end.

continues

35

Drawing *(continued)*

Drawing Rectangles and Squares

Select the Rectangle tool. Click where you want the upper left corner of the rectangle; then drag the mouse to where you want the lower right corner of the rectangle. Hold down the Shift key if you want to draw a square.

Drawing Ellipses and Circles

Select the Ellipse tool. Next pretend to draw an invisible rectangle that just fits the ellipse by clicking on one corner of the rectangle and then dragging the mouse to the opposite corner of the rectangle. Hold down the Shift key if you want to draw a circle.

Drawing Arcs

Select the Arc tool. Click where you want the arc line to start; then drag the mouse to where you want the arc line to end. If you want a 90-degree arc, hold down the Shift key as you drag the mouse.

Drawing Wild, Freeform Shapes

Select the Freeform tool. Draw a series of squiggle-y lines by dragging the mouse, and draw straight lines as described above. Double-click the mouse to close the shape.

Coloring Drawn Objects

Use the Fill Color toolbar button to change the interior colors of drawn objects.

Use the Line Color toolbar button to change the border line color of drawn objects.

When you select either tool, a box of colored buttons is displayed. You simply click the color you want.

Changing Line Style and Thickness

 Use the Line Style tool to change the appearance and thickness of the lines you draw to create any object.

When you select the tool, a list box of line styles is displayed. You can guess how this works, right? You simply select the line style that looks like what you want.

Moving Objects

You can move any object by selecting it and then dragging it.

 You can restack objects that you've intentionally (or unintentionally) dog-piled on each other too. Use the Send to Back tool to restack the dog-piled objects so that the selected object is at the bottom of the pile.

 Use the Bring to Front tool to restack the dog-piled objects so that the selected object is at the top of the pile.

Defining dog pile

You remember what a dog pile is, right? Inexplicably, a bunch of 7-year-olds decide it'll be fun to all pile on top of one another. One kid jumps on another kid's back, and these two fall to the ground. Next other kids start jumping on the two kids that are already down. If you start drawing objects on top of one another, you don't get the grass stains, of course, but you do get a dog-pile of sorts.

Resizing Objects

You can resize drawn objects by selecting them and then dragging the selection handles. The selection handles are those little black squares that Word uses to mark the selected object.

Placing Objects Behind and in Front of Text

 You can move an object so that it's in front of text by choosing the Bring in Front of Text tool.

 If you later want to move the object so that it's behind text, select the Send Behind Text tool.

continues

Drawing *(continued)*

Grouping Objects

 You can group drawn objects so that editing changes that you make to one of the objects in the group also get made to the other objects. To do this, select the Select Drawing Objects tool; then click and drag the mouse to draw a rectangle that includes all the objects you want to group.

 After you select all the objects in the group, select the Group tool.

Ungrouping Objects

 To ungroup previously grouped objects, select the group. Then select the Ungroup tool.

Flipping Objects

 You can flip drawn objects horizontally or vertically. To flip a drawn object horizontally, select it and then use the Flip Horizontal tool.

 To flip a drawn object vertically, select it and then use the Flip Vertical tool.

Rotating Objects

 You can rotate the selected object 90 degrees by selecting the Rotate Right tool.

Reshaping Objects

 To change the shape of a freeform object, select it, select the Reshape tool, and then drag the selection handles that Word adds.

Using a Snap-to Grid for Object Placement

 To add a grid of horizontal and vertical lines that you can use to align and position objects, select the Snap-to-Grid tool.

Creating a Picture

 To turn an object into a picture so that text can wrap around it select the object and and then select the Create Picture tool.

Aligning Objects

To vertically or horizontally align the selected object, select the Align Drawing Objects tool. Then, when Word displays the Align dialog box, select the horizontal and vertical alignment you want.

Where objects align

When Word aligns a single drawn object, it aligns the object against the page edge. A left-aligned circle, for example, is placed next to the left edge of the page. Note that this differs from the against-the-margin alignment used for text.

Drop-and-Drag I think this is the name of a TV show about hunting. It's on one of the cable stations. I mention this only so you don't confuse the TV show with the similarly named Word feature, **Drag-and-Drop.**

Dropped Caps A dropped capital letter is sometimes used as the first letter in a document.

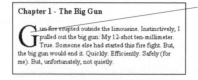

You often see dropped capital letters at the start of mystery novels.

You can drop cap the selected character using the Format Drop Cap command.

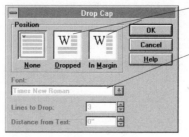

Select either the Dropped or In Margin option.

You can specify some other, different font, pick a drop depth in lines, and specify how far from the text the drop letter should be placed.

Changing Fonts; Fonts

Editing Tables The cells in tables are easy to edit.

Replacing Cell Contents

Click in the cell near the left cell edge. Word selects the entire cell's contents. You can replace the contents by typing.

Editing Cell Contents

Click inside the cell where you want to place the **insertion point**. Then edit the cell contents in the usual way. You know what I mean. Typing, deleting, backspacing, and so forth. Enough said.

Editing Text

To edit text you've already entered, first select the character or the block of text you want to change. (You can do this by clicking just before the first character you want to change and then dragging the mouse to just after the last character you want to change.) Next type the new text you want to replace the old text.

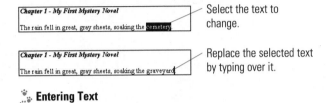

Chapter 1 - My First Mystery Novel

The rain fell in great, gray sheets, soaking the cemetery

Select the text to change.

Chapter 1 - My First Mystery Novel

The rain fell in great, gray sheets, soaking the graveyard

Replace the selected text by typing over it.

Entering Text

Overtyping

Normally, Word inserts the characters you type at the **insertion point** location. You can tell Word to replace, or overtype, characters that follow the insertion point by pressing the Insert key. Word bolds the OVR indicator on the status bar when you do. Any text you type will replace existing text, starting with the character just right of the insertion point. To turn off overtype, press the Insert key again.

Embedding and Linking Existing Objects
To create an object from an existing file, follow these steps:

1 Choose the Insert Object command.

2 Select the Create from File tab.

3 Describe the object file location.

4 Identify the object file.

5 Mark the Link to File check box if Windows should update the object for subsequent file changes.

6 Mark the Display as Icon check box if Word should display an icon rather than a picture.

7 Select OK.

❖ Object Linking and Embedding

Embedding New Objects
To create an object from scratch using an application other than Word, follow these steps:

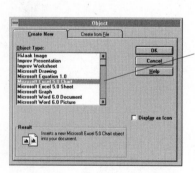

1 Choose the Insert Object command.

2 Select the Create New tab.

3 Select the Windows application that creates the object.

4 Mark the Display as Icon check box to see an icon rather than as a picture.

5 Select OK. Word starts the selected application, allowing you to create the object.

❖ Object Linking and Embedding

End-of-Document Markers Under the last line of **documents** in the Normal and Outline document views, Word places a thick, quarter-inch long underline character. This character, which is called the end-of-document marker, identifies your document's last line.

Do you even care about all this? Maybe not. But this bit of trivia isn't entirely worthless. If you've got extra blank pages printing at the end of each and every document, it may be that you've accumulated paragraph breaks at the end of the document and are printing the paragraph breaks. In this case, the end-of-document marker won't be under your last line of text; it'll be separated from that line by a bunch of empty lines.

☙ **Document Views**

Ending Lines You normally don't have to worry about ending lines of text. Word automatically **word wraps** your lines. If you want to end a line of text without ending a **paragraph**, however, you can do so by pressing Shift+Enter.

☙ **Paragraphs; Word Wrap**

Endnotes In Word you add, modify, and delete end notes the same as you do footnotes.

☙ **Footnote and Endnote Options; Footnotes and Endnotes**

Entering Text To enter text into a **document**, you simply use the keyboard to type the **characters**. Tap, tap, tap. No joke. That's all there is to it.

☙ **Copying Text**

continues

Entering Text *(continued)*

Carriage returns

Don't press Enter (the Return key) at the ends of lines; Word moves the **insertion point** to the next line when it runs out of room. Word also moves words from one line to the next line if there isn't room. This feature is called **word wrap**.

Envelopes You can print an envelope with Word as long as your printer accepts envelopes. All you need to do is stick the envelope into your printer the way it expects it. If you're typing a label that shows the person's name and address, select these. Then choose the Tools Envelopes and Labels command, and select the Envelope page tab.

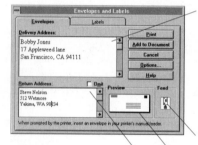

Enter the name and the address of the person to whom you want the post office to deliver your letter. Word fills this block with whatever you selected, so you may not need to change the Delivery Address block.

The Feed box shows how to stick the envelope into the printer.

The Preview box shows how your envelope will look.

If you're not using pre-printed envelopes that already show your return address, use the Return Address block to provide this information. If you don't want to print the return address, mark the Omit check box.

When you're ready, select Print. Word prints your envelope.

Erasing

You can erase the current selection—a character, a **paragraph**, a picture, a **table,** or some combination of these document parts—by pressing the Del key or choosing Edit Clear.

You can erase the preceding **character** or the current selection by pressing Backspace.

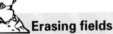

Erasing fields

You can't Backspace over fields—even when a field includes a single character. So, to erase a field, you need to select the entire field and then press Del or choose Edit Clear. If you don't know what a field is (or, at least, what a Word "field" is), don't worry. Your document probably doesn't have any. But, just so you know, a field is simply an instruction to Word to insert something into your document.

Erasing Documents

Documents are files stored on disk. To erase them, therefore, you use either the Windows File Manager application or the MS-DOS Del or Erase commands. For information about how to use the File Manager or MS-DOS to erase a document file, refer to the user documentation that came with your copy of Windows or MS-DOS.

If you accidentally erase a document

You should know that it may be possible to recover, or unerase, a document file. How you unerase files is beyond the scope of this little book, but if you've just erased a document that you now realize you desperately need, stop what you're doing. Don't save anything else to your hard disk. And look up the File Undelete command in the MS-DOS user documentation.

Exiting Word
To exit from Word—or just about any other Windows application—you can choose the File Exit command. Or you can close the Word application window—for example, by double-clicking on its Control-menu box. Word will ask if you want to save documents that have unsaved changes.

> ⁘ **Closing Documents; Saving Documents; Windows Command Buttons**

Exporting Documents
Exporting means copying a document so that you or some friend can use it with another program—usually another word-processor application such as WordPerfect. You export a Word document by saving the file in a format the other program can use.

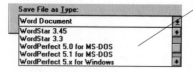

Save File as **T**ype:
Word Document
WordStar 3.45
WordStar 3.3
WordPerfect 5.0 for MS-DOS
WordPerfect 5.1 for MS-DOS
WordPerfect 5.x for Windows

To export a document file, save the file in a format that the other program can open.

> ⁘ **Saving Documents; WordPerfect**

Choosing an export file format
If you can't find a file format that matches the application to which you want to export the document, use one of the text file formats. In this case, you may not be able to export the document formatting, but you will be able to export the document text.

Field Codes
Field codes are really instructions that you've entered (or that Word has entered) into a **document**. This sounds complicated, but it's not.

Entering Field Codes
You enter field codes into documents using the Insert Field Command. You enter field codes, for example, to direct Word to add a term to the **index** or a heading to the **table of contents**. And you enter field codes to direct Word to calculate **formulas**.

Viewing Field Codes
To see the field codes in a document—usually Word shows the field results—choose the Tools Options command, select the View tab, and then mark the Show Field Codes check box.

Figure Captions
Do you ever put figures in your documents? If you do and you want to tag the figures with captions, use the Insert Caption command, which, in essence, lets you connect captions to the figures they describe.

Adding Figure Captions
To add a caption to a figure, select the figure, choose the Insert Caption command, and then follow these steps:

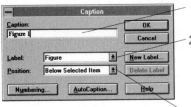

1 Enter the caption into the Caption text box.

2 Identify what you're labeling as either a figure, a table, or an equation in the Label drop-down list box.

3 Specify the caption placement using the Position drop-down list box.

File Names

You give a **document** its file name when you choose the File Save As command.

File Name Rules

MS-DOS file-naming rules apply to Word document files. A file name can't contain more than eight characters. All numbers and letters that appear on your keyboard are OK. And so are many other characters. You can't, however, use characters that MS-DOS expects to be used in special ways on its command line, such as spaces, asterisks, and question marks. If you need more information than this, refer to the MS-DOS user documentation that almost surely came with your computer.

Specifying File Extensions

The MS-DOS file extension, by the way, isn't something you need to worry about. Word uses file extensions to identify file type. You can accept the default Microsoft Word document file type, DOC. Or you can use the File Save As dialog box's File Type drop-down list box to select some other file type.

Save Options; Saving Documents

File Summary

In addition to the **text,** pictures, and **tables** stored in a **document**, you can store additional information that describes the document itself and makes it easier to find. You collect and store this additional information by filling out the Summary Info dialog box, which Word displays when you choose the File Summary Info command.

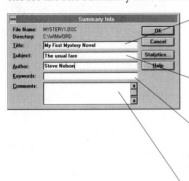

Give a lengthy, full, descriptive title to your document using the Title text box.

Identify the document subject matter and author.

Add keywords that will make it easy to later find the document file using the File Find File command.

Describe additional information about the document file in the Comments box.

Finding Formatting

You can search for formatting. Simply follow these steps:

1 Choose the Edit Find command. Word dutifully displays the Find dialog box.

2 Select the Format command button. Word lists the types of formatting.

3 Select a formatting type from the list. Word displays another dialog box.

4 Describe the type of formatting you're looking for.

Sure. This all sounds rather cumbersome, but it's not all that difficult if you're looking for formatting you assigned.

⁙ Finding Text

Finding Lost Documents

You can use the File Find File command to locate documents based on characteristics of the file and summary information collected about the file. For step-by-step information on how to use this command to find a lost document, refer to **Troubleshooting: You Can't Find a Document.**

Finding Text

Choose the Edit Find command to locate words, phrases, and other fragments of **text** in a **document**. To use the Edit Find command, select the document area Word should search, or don't select anything if you want Word to search the entire document. Then choose the Edit Find command.

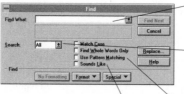

In the Find What text box, specify what it is you're looking for.

Use the Search drop-down list box to indicate in which direction Word should search, or look.

Use the Match Case and Find Whole Words Only check boxes to indicate whether Word should consider case (lower vs. upper) in its search and look for whole words rather than partial words.

Use the Sounds Like check box to find words that are pronounced like the Find What text: their and there, you're and your, are and our, and so on. You get the idea, right?

Find Next starts and re-starts the search.

⁙ Finding Formatting; Replacing Text

Footers Page footers can be added to the bottom of printed documents.

   Headers and Footers

Footnote and Endnote Options Word gives you quite a bit of control over where and how it locates footnotes and endnotes and how it numbers these notes. To exercise this control, you choose the Options command button when the Footnote and Endnote dialog box appears. (In case you've forgotten or never knew, the Footnote and Endnote dialog box appears when you choose the Insert Footnote command.)

1 Select either the All Footnotes or the All Endnotes tab to tell Word which type of note you're going to noodle around with. Both tab options look and work just about the same, by the way.

2 Use the Place At drop-down list box to tell Word where notes go. You've got different options for footnotes and endnotes, but all the placement options are self-explanatory.

3 Use the Number Format drop-down list box to select a numbering scheme. You can choose regular arabic numbers (1, 2, 3, . . .), roman numerals (i, ii, iii, . . .), alphabetic lettering (a, b, c, . . .), or symbols (*, †,‡,...).

4 Use the Start At option to tell Word which footnote or endnote number to use first.

5 Use the Numbering radio buttons to tell Word if and where it should restart the numbering.

   Footnotes and Endnotes

Footnotes and Endnotes
A footnote appears at the bottom of the page. An endnote appears at the very end of the **document**.

Adding Footnotes and Endnotes

Move the **insertion point** to the place in your text where the footnote or endnote marker should be placed. (The marker is probably the footnote or the endnote number.) Then choose the Insert Footnote command.

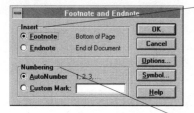

Tell Word whether you want the note to appear at the foot of the page as a footnote or at the end of the document or document **section** as an endnote.

Use the Numbering radio buttons to specify how footnotes should be marked. Select the AutoNumber button if they should be numbered. (This is the usual case.) Or, if you want to use some other **character** (such as an asterisk), enter the character in the Custom Mark text box.

Press Enter when the Insert Footnote dialog box describes how you want to add the footnote. Word opens the footnote pane and moves the insertion point to it so that you can type your footnote.

All Footnotes	Close

[1] This is footnote sure enough. It appears in something called the footnote pane. The footnote pane is just a separate chunk of the document window used to--you guessed it--show your footnotes.

Deleting Footnotes and Endnotes

To delete a footnote or an endnote, select the footnote or endnote marker. (This is probably the note number unless you're someone who needs to have it your way and, so, assigned a custom note marker.)
Then press Del.

🐾 **Footnote and Endnote Options**

About note numbering

When you delete a footnote or an endnote and you've used the default autonumbering, Word renumbers the remaining document footnotes or endnotes after the deletion.

Fonts   Word lets you use a wide variety of fonts in your documents. With fonts, you can even add Greek symbols and other special characters to your document. Here are a few examples:

Arial resembles Helvetica.

Braggadocio is, well, rather bold.

Courier New looks like typewriter output.

DESDEMONA IS REALLY RATHER FUNKY, DON'T YOU AGREE?

Times New Roman uses serifs—little cross strokes—to make characters easier to read.

ΑΣΔΦαβχψυσΩΙΥ   These are **TrueType** Symbol characters.

♊♏♒&♏♐◻※⊠❖⌘●&er♞✿♱   These are TrueType Wingding characters.

🐾 **Changing Fonts**

Form Letters ❖ Mail Merge

Format Painting ❖ Copying Formatting

Formatting

Borders—**Paragraph Borders**	
Changing character font and point size—**Changing Fonts**	
Changing character spacing—**Character Spacing**	
Creating format combinations—**Creating Styles**	
Horizontal Alignment—**Indenting and Alignment**	
Page margins—**Margins**	
Pagination and paragraphs—**Text Flow**	
Replacing styles—**Changing Styles**	
Searching for formatting—**Finding Formatting**	
Shading—**Paragraph Borders**	
Spacing —**Paragraph and Line Spacing**	
Text around pictures—**Frames**	

Formula Functions Functions are prefabricated formulas. In Word, you can use functions in your table formulas.

Using Functions in Formulas

To use a function, choose the Table Formula command, tell Word which formula you want to calculate by selecting the function from the Paste Function drop-down list, and then supply the function input values separated by commas.

Reviewing Word's Functions

Word provides 18 functions. If yours is an inquiring mind that needs to know, review the list that follows:

Function	Purpose
ABS	Returns the absolute number of the input value. For example, the function =ABS(-3) returns 3.
AND	Lets you perform a compound "AND" logic test. For example, the function =AND(1=1,2+2=4) returns 1 because both logical tests are true.
AVERAGE	Calculates the arithmetic mean, or average, of the input values. For example, the function =AVERAGE(1,2,3,4) returns 2.5.
COUNT	Counts the input values. For example, the function =COUNT(1,2,3,4,5,6) returns 6.
DEFINED	Determines whether a formula can be calculated, returning 1 if the formula can be calculated and 0 if it can't. For example, the function =DEFINED(1/0) returns 0 because you can't divide the zero.
FALSE	Returns the logical value for false, 0. For example, =FALSE returns 0.
IF	Performs a logical test and returns one result if test is true and another if test is false. For example, =IF(2+2=4,1,0) returns the value 1, proving once and for all that 2+2 does indeed equal 4.
INT	Returns the integer portion of a value. For example, =INT(3.5) returns 3.
MAX	Returns the largest input value. For example, the function =MAX(1,2,3,4) returns 4.
MIN	Returns the smallest input value. For example, the function =MIN(1,2,3,4) returns 1.
MOD	Returns the modulus, or remainder, left over from a division operation. For example, the function =MOD(3,2) returns 1 because that's what gets left over when you divide 3 by 2.
NOT	Lets you perform a compound "NOT" logic test. For example, the function =NOT(1=1,2+2=4) returns 0 because both logical tests are true.

continues

Formula Functions *(continued)*

Function	Purpose
OR	Lets you perform a compound "OR" logic test. For example, the function =OR(1>1,2+2=4) returns 1 because the second logical test is true.
PRODUCT	Multiplies the function arguments by each other. For example, =PRODUCT(2,3,4) returns 24.
ROUND	Rounds an input value to a specified decimal precision. For example, ROUND(123.456,2) returns 123.46.
SIGN	Returns -1 if the input value is a negative value, a 1 if the input value is a positive value, and 0 if the input value is 0. For example, =SIGN(-3) returns -1.
SUM	Sums the input values. For example, +SUM(2,2) returns 4.
TRUE	Returns the logical value for true, 1. For example, =TRUE returns 1.

Formulas

Word's functions closely resemble Excel's functions

Word's formula functions work like a spreadsheet's functions. If you've used Microsoft Excel's functions, you'll find using Word's functions easy and straightforward.

Formulas When Henry David Thoreau wrote *Walden*, he included a table like the one shown below that totaled his cabin construction costs.

Boards	8.03½
Refuse shingles	4.00
Laths	1.25
Two second hand windows	2.43
Glass	4.00
One thousand old brick	2.40
Two casks of lime	0.31
Hair	0.15
Mantle-tree iron	3.90
Nails	0.14
Hinges and screws	0.10
Latch	0.01
Chalk	1.40
In all (the total)	28.12½

Adding AutoSum Formulas

If you write a book about living in the woods and need to summarize your cabin costs, use a Word formula. Simply build a **table,** select the cell where the total formula should go, and choose the Insert Formula command. If you want to total the cells in a table, select OK.

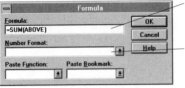

You can choose to make another calculation by entering a function.

You can also format the formula result by choosing an entry from this list box.

Writing Your Own Formulas

You can type any formula into the Formula text box and have Word place the formula result into the selected table cell. Begin the formula with the = sign and use the arithmetic operators: + for addition, - for subtraction, * for multiplication, / for division, and ^ for exponentiation. Override standard arithmetic operator precedence rules by using parentheses.

Using Cell Addresses

You can also use table cell addresses in a formula, in which case Word uses the value in the referenced cell. Table cell addresses consist of the column letter and row number. Table columns are lettered A, B, C, and so on. Table rows are numbered 1, 2, 3, and so on. So, table cell A1 is the cell in the upper left corner of the table.

Recalculating Formulas Because Inputs Change

You can recalculate a table formula when an input to the formula changes. Select the cell with the formula; then press F9.

 Functions

More on formulas

You can also use prefabricated formulas, called functions, by selecting a function from the Paste Function list box.

Fractions

You can enter fraction characters—¼, ½, and ¾ —into documents. You can also create reasonable-looking fractions using numbers and the slash key.

Using Fraction Symbols

To use a fraction character, choose the Insert Symbol command, select normal text in the Font drop-down list box, and then click on the fraction you want. When you use the Insert Symbol command, your fraction is actually a single character.

Creating Fractions from Scratch

If you want to get tricky, you can create a fraction that looks pretty good by reducing the point size for the numbers and the slash characters (as compared with what you're using elsewhere in the document), making the numerator a superscript character and the denominator a subscript character, as in 3/8. When you use the superscript and subscript approach, your fraction is actually a combination of smaller-than-normal characters.

 Changing Fonts; Symbols

Frames

You should know about frames. Here's why. You can use frames to, in essence, block out a chunk of page space so that the blocked-out, or framed, space isn't used for text. When you do this, Word will rearrange the text so that it flows around the frame.

Chapter 13 - Smorgasbord

I squatted in the tall grass. I tried not to move. The lion might choose some other entree. Would not a fleet-footed antelope be more sporting? A bit of exercise before lunch had always appealed to me.

I decided to try another approach. Softly, I began whispering, "Nice kitty, nice kitty." The big cat meowed. I was safe.

You can wrap text around frames. Even poorly written fiction.

Adding a Frame

To add a frame to an object, select the object and choose the Insert Frame command. Word prompts you to switch to the Page Layout view. To see text wrapped around a frame, choose the View Page Layout command. You move and resize frames the same way you move and resize pictures.

Moving Pictures; Resizing Pictures

Full Screen

You can use almost all of your screen to display a **document.** When you view a document in a full screen, Word displays only the document. Word doesn't display the menu bar, the toolbars, or the title bars of the **application window** and the **document window.**

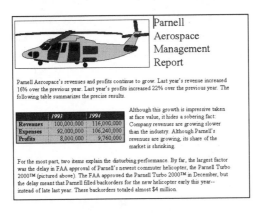

Viewing the Full Screen

To view the Word application window as a full screen, choose the View Full Screen command.

Viewing the Regular Screen

To return to the regular view of the application window, choose the Full button that Word displays whenever you've gone "full screen."

continues

Full Screen *(continued)*

Choosing commands when you're in full-screen view

Even though the menu bar doesn't show when you're using the full-screen view of the Word application window, you can still activate menus so that they display their commands, and then you can choose commands. All you have to do is use the keyboard to activate the menu. For example, you can press Alt+F to activate the File menu. The character you press along with the Alt key to activate a menu is underlined in the menu name.

Functions Word provides many of the same calculation functions as does its spreadsheet cousin, Microsoft Excel.

To use a function, you first build the table that'll hold the values and the function formulas. Then you choose the Table Formula command and select its Paste Function box. If you've worked with Excel a bit, you'll find this function business easy to understand and use.

⁘ **Formula Functions; Formulas**

Go To You can choose the Edit Go To command to move the **insertion point.**

Use the Go To What list box and the Enter Page Number text box to describe where you want the insertion point moved. As you select different document parts—pages, sections, lines, bookmarks, and so on—Word renames the text box to correspond to the selected entry.

Grammar Checking

Choose the Tools Grammar command to check the grammar of a document or the selected sentences or paragraphs in a document. (If you want to check an entire document, you don't select anything.) When you choose the command, Word begins reviewing your sentences. If it finds a kooky sentence, it displays the Grammar dialog box.

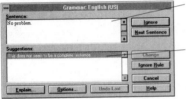

Word shows the suspicious sentence here.

Oh, oh. An incomplete sentence. No problem. I can fix that.

⁙ **Grammar Checking Options**

Grammar Checking Options

Word lets you select a writing style and then apply an appropriate set of grammar and usage rules. To do this, choose the Tools Options command and then select the Grammar tab.

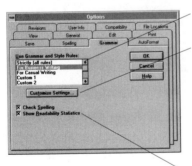

Use the list box to select a writing style.

If you want to adjust or change specific grammar and usage rules, select this command button. Word displays a dialog box you use to mark very specific decisions about how Word should check grammar.

Mark these check boxes if Word should also check spelling and calculate some readability statistics.

⁙ **Readability**

Graphs

Word comes with the Microsoft Graph application. Graph, as it's called by those who know it well, lets you easily add charts to your Word **documents**.

Describing the To-Be-Plotted Data

The easiest way to describe the data you want to plot in a graph is to create a **table** that holds the data. To do this, follow these steps:

1 Choose the Table Insert Table command to add a table to the document.

2 Fill the table rows with descriptions of what you want to plot as well as the actual data.

Sales	125	135	150	170	200
Profits	-5	5	10	20	30

Plotting Data

Once you've created a table with the data you want to show in a graph, you're ready to chart the data. To do this, follow these steps:

1 Select the table.

2 Select the Insert Chart tool. The Microsoft Graph application starts and draws a column chart in its **application window**.

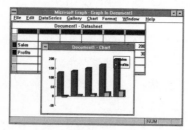

Microsoft Graph uses two document windows

You'll see two document windows in the Graph application window: One shows the graph, and the other, called a datasheet, shows the table. You can edit the table data using the datasheet document window.

Moving the Legend

The legend, which identifies the data you've plotted, initially appears inside the plot area—usually on top of the chart. You can move it by clicking it (to select it) and then dragging it to a new location.

Choosing a Chart Type

Although Graph chooses an initial chart type for you—a 3-dimensional column chart—you can easily choose another chart type simply by choosing a chart type command from the Gallery menu. When you do, Graph shows pictures of the chart type formatted in slightly different ways. You can select a chart type and format simply by clicking it.

Reviewing Graph's 12 Chart Types

Graph supplies 12 chart types, which you choose by using the Gallery menu commands. Which type you use depends on the visual comparison you want.

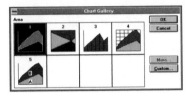

An area chart plots data series as cumulative lines. The first data series values are plotted in a line. Then the second data series values are plotted in a line that gets stacked on top of the first line. Then the third data series values get stacked on top of the second line, and so on.

continues

Graphs *(continued)*

Defining the term *data series*

A data series is simply a set of related values plotted with the same **data marker** in an Microsoft Graph chart. If you find the term *data series* confusing, you can use a sneaky trick to identify the data series that a chart plots. Ask yourself, "What am I plotting?" Every one-word answer will identify a data series. For example, if you ask the "What am I plotting?" question about a chart that plots sales revenue over 5 years, you can answer, "Sales." Sales then is a data series. By the way, the data markers that visually represent the sales set of values will all look similar. For example, the sales data series might be depicted with a set of red bars or as points along the same line.

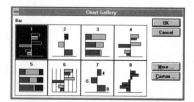

A Bar chart plots each data series values using horizontal bars. Good for comparing individual values when the chart category isn't time.

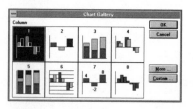

A Column chart is like a bar chart, but it plots each data series values as vertical bars. Good for comparing individual values when the chart category is time.

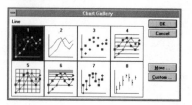

A Line chart plots each data series values as points on a line. Emphasizes trends in the data series values.

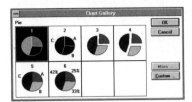

A Pie chart plots a single data series with each value in the series represented as a pie slice. Probably the least effective chart type available because you're technically limited to a single data series and practically limited to a small number of values. (Otherwise you slice the pie into too many pieces.)

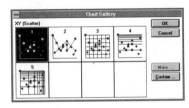

An XY, or Scatter, chart uses two value axes gridlines to plot pairs of data points in a line. Because it visually shows the correlation between two data series, this is the most powerful and useful chart type available.

Defining the term *chart gridlines*

Chart gridlines make it easier to calibrate the values plotted in a chart and to differentiate the categories. Category axis gridlines extend perpendicularly from the category axis—and help you keep the data categories straight. Value axis gridlines extend perpendicularly from the value axis—and help you more easily calibrate plotted values.

continues

G

Graphs *(continued)*

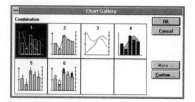

A Combination chart combines two other chart types by using two types of markers—such as columns and lines. Often times, you can create hybrid charts to show different aspects of the different data sets. For example, you can use column markers for one data series to emphasize absolute values and then use a line for another data series to emphasize trends.

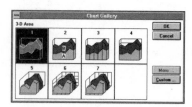

Like its 2-dimensional cousin, the 3-D Area chart plots data series with lines and then colors the area between the lines. Note that some of the 3-D area chart autoformats use the third dimension of depth to organize the data series.

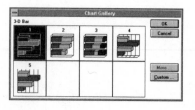

A 3-D Bar chart plots each data series values using horizontal solid bars. Good for comparing individual values when the chart category isn't time—but a bit imprecise.

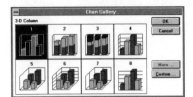

A 3-D Column chart plots each data series values as solid vertical bars. Note that some of the 3-D column chart autoformats use the third dimension of depth to organize the data series. Like the 3-D bar chart, a bit imprecise.

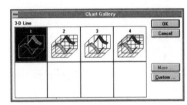

A 3-D Line chart should probably be called a ribbon chart. It plots each data series values as points on a ribbon. Emphasizes trends in the data series values, but tricky to use. (The ribbon's three-dimensionality makes it difficult to accurately gauge how fast the line rises or falls.)

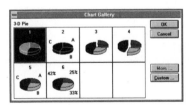

A 3-D Pie chart plots a single data series with each value in the series represented as a pie wedge in a solid cylinder. Extremely difficult to use well. (Pie wedges in the chart background appear smaller than same-sized pie wedges in the foreground.)

continues

Graphs *(continued)*

Adding, Moving, and Removing Chart Titles

To add text that describes a chart and its data, use the Chart Titles command. When Graph displays a dialog box that in effect asks for the type of text you want to add, select the appropriate radio button, select OK, and then type the text you want.

Once you've added a title to a chart, you can move the text you add by selecting it and dragging.

You can remove a chart title by selecting it and pressing Del.

Adding and Removing Data Labels

To label a chart's markers with the plotted values or percentages, use the Chart Data Labels command. When Graph displays a dialog box that in effect asks for the type of data label you want to add, select the appropriate radio button and OK. (In general, you only add percentage labels to pie charts.)

You can remove data labels by choosing the Chart Data Labels command, marking None, and then selecting OK.

Adding, Moving, and Removing Arrows

To add an arrow to a chart—perhaps to point out some subtlety in the plotted data—use the Chart Add Arrow command. When you choose this command, Graph adds an arrow.

To move the arrow that Graph adds, drag it.

To remove the arrow, select it, and then choose the Chart Delete Arrow command. (Graph replaces the Chart Add Arrow command with the Chart Delete Arrow command if the selected object is an arrow.)

Adding and Removing Legends

A legend identifies the data you've plotted. You can remove a legend by choosing the Chart Delete Legend command. Or, if a chart doesn't already have a legend, you can add one by choosing the Chart Add Legend command.

Legend names

If you organize your to-be-plotted data into rows, Graph uses the contents of the first cell in the row to name the data in the legend.

Adding and Removing Axes

If you don't need an axis to calibrate, or organize, the plotted data, you can use the Chart Axes command to add and remove axes. When you choose this command, Graph displays a dialog box with check boxes you use to turn on and off the display of vertical, horizontal, and—in the case of a 3-dimensional chart—depth axes.

Adding and Removing Gridlines

Graph will add vertical and horizontal gridlines to the plot area. Sometimes, these gridlines make it easier for chart viewers to calibrate the chart markers. To add and remove gridlines from one of your charts, you can use the Chart Gridlines command. There's nothing complicated about doing this. When you choose this command, Graph displays a dialog box with check boxes you use to turn on and off the display of vertical and horizontal gridlines.

continues

Graphs (continued)

Formatting the Chart

The Format menu provides a series of commands you can use to change the way the parts of your chart look. In general, the way you do this is by selecting the chart part you want to change and then choosing a command.

Returning to the Word Document

Once you finish choosing a chart type and making any other changes to the graph, choose the File Exit command. Windows stops the Graph application and returns you to the Word document, which will now show the new chart.

∴ **Tables; Embedding New Objects**

Headers and Footers

Headers and footers appear in the top and bottom margins of pages and usually describe some aspect of the printed page or document—such as the page number.

You can use a different header or footer for the first page in a document. And you can use different headers and footers for each document section.

Adding a Header or a Footer

Choose the View Header and Footer command. Word changes the document view to show laid-out pages. It also draws a dashed line in the top and bottom margins of pages to show where the header or footer goes.

```
Header
```

You can type whatever you want in the header or footer box.

Using the Header and Footer Toolbar

You can use the Header and Footer toolbar to build your headers and footers too:

Tool	Description
	Flip-flops between the page's header and footer
	Shows previous page header or footer
	Shows the next page header or footer
	Tells Word to make this page's header or footer the same as the previous one
	Adds a page number to header or footer
	Adds a date to header or footer
	Adds a time to header or footer

continues

Headers and Footers *(continued)*

Tool	Description
	Displays the Page Setup dialog box
	Hides and unhides the document text
Close	Closes the header or footer box and removes the toolbar

Document Views

Help

Need help with some Microsoft Word task? No problem. Select the Help tool. Word adds a question mark to the mouse pointer.

To indicate what you want help with, click the menu command, a toolbar button, or part of a window other than text. After you select the item you want help with, Word starts the Help application, and it displays any specific information about what you selected.

Hyphenation

You can use hyphens to minimize the raggedness of the right margin. To do this, choose the Tools Hyphenation command.

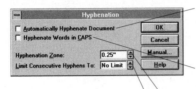

Mark the Automatically Hyphenate Document check box to hyphenate words as you enter them.

Mark the Hyphenate Words In CAPS box if it's OK to hyphenate all words that use all capital letters.

Use the Hyphenation Zone box to specify how close to the right margin edge words can end.

Use the Limit Consecutive Hyphens To box to tell Word how many lines in a row can end with hyphens.

Suppressing hyphenation

You can tell Word that it shouldn't hyphenate the selected paragraph. To do this, choose the Format Paragraph command, select the Text Flow tab, and mark the Don't Hyphenate check box.

Importing Documents

You can open documents created by other word-processor programs. You can also import any ASCII text file. To do this, choose the File Open command. Then use the List Files of Types list box to identify the to-be-imported file's format. After you've done this, open the file by describing its location, using the Drives and Directories list boxes, and its name, using the File Name box.

Indenting and Alignment

You can change paragraph indenting and alignment using the Format Paragraph command. An indention is the space between the page margin edge and the place a line of characters starts or must end. Paragraph alignment refers to how the lines of text appear between the left and right margins.

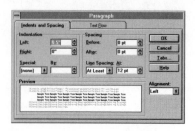

1 Use the Left and Right boxes to specify the indenting in inches.

2 Use the Special and By combo boxes to specify indenting only for the first line of a paragraph.

3 Use the Alignment drop-down list to specify how the paragraph should be horizontally aligned: Left (against the left margin), Right (against the right margin), Centered (between the margins), or Justified (spaced so that lines begin and end exactly at the left and right margins).

 Paragraph and Line Spacing

Index

An index is simply an alphabetized list of the terms used in a document. It's usually a very handy tool for readers. (That's why we put one in this book, for example—to make using this book easier for you.) You can add indexes to your documents.

Adding an index is a two-part process. The first part of the process is telling Word which terms belong in your index. The second part of the process is telling Word to build the index using your index entries.

Adding Index Entries

1 Select a term.

2 Choose the Insert Index and Tables command (so that Word displays the Indexes and Tables dialog box).

3 Select the Mark Entry command button (so that Word displays the Mark Index Entry dialog box).

4 Word leaves the Mark Index Entry dialog box open. You can add additional terms to your index by scrolling through your document and then selecting terms and the Mark command button.

Index field codes

As you mark each index entry, Word adds the index entry field code following the word. If you tell Word to add the term "Document" to your index, it adds the field code {XE "Document"} to your document. You will see this code only if the Show/Hide button is pressed on the Standard toolbar.

continues

Index *(continued)*

Adding the Index

Choose the Insert Index and Tables command so that Word displays the Index and Tables dialog box.

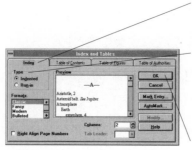

Select the Index page tab if it isn't already displayed.

Choose the type and format for your index. The Preview box shows what the index will look like with the choices you've made.

Select OK to generate the index. Word will look through your document, finding each of the index entry field codes. Whenever it finds one, it'll add the term to your index.

About indexes

There's more to the mechanics of index creation than I've described here. What's more, good indexing is an art. Therefore, if you get into this indexing business, let me offer a couple of suggestions. First, consider reviewing the discussion of indexing in the Word user documentation. Or, get a tutorial that covers indexing in painstaking detail. Second, start looking at the indexes in books like this one. You can learn a lot by reviewing the work of a professional indexer (such as the woman who indexed this book).

Insertion Point The insertion point is the vertical bar that shows where what you type gets placed. If you can't figure this out, start Word, begin typing, and look at the bar that moves ahead of the text you type. See it? That's the insertion point.

Italic Characters To *italicize* **characters,** select them and then press Ctrl+I or select the Italicize tool. You can also use the Format Font command.

Kerning ❖ Character Spacing

Line Numbers You can number the lines in a document **section**. To do this, choose the File Page Setup command, select the Layout tab, and click the Line Numbers command button.

Suppressing line numbers

You can format a paragraph so that it doesn't show line numbers even if you've told Word to number all the lines in a document section. To do this, select the paragraph and choose the Format Paragraph command. Then select the Text Flow tab and mark the Suppress Line Numbers check box.

Line Spacing ❖ Paragraph and Line Spacing

Macro A macro is simply a list of commands. This doesn't sound very exciting, of course. And maybe it isn't. But Word lets you store these lists and repeat, or play back, the stored keystrokes and mouse clicks. With this play-back ability, you can automate operations that work the same way every time they're performed. For more information on macros, see your Word user documentation.

Mail Merge
Word will produce form letters, mailing labels, and other similar documents by extracting information from a database of names and addresses and then using this information to "fill in the blanks" of a standard document.

Creating the Main Mail Merge Document

You need to create a special merge document, but this is very simple. Follow these steps:

1 Choose the Tools Merge Mail command. Word displays the Mail Merge Helper dialog box.

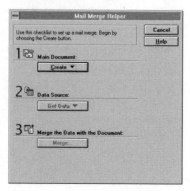

2 Select the Create command button. Word displays a list of mail merge document types: form letters, mailing labels, envelopes, and catalog.

3 Select a mail merge document type—such as Form Letters.

4 When Word asks, indicate if you want to make the active document a mail merge document or want to create a new, blank mail merge document.

Your next task is to identify the database that will supply the information used to create the mail merge document.

Creating Your Mail Merge Database Inside Word

1 Choose the Tools Mail Merge command. Word displays the Mail Merge Helper dialog box.

2 Select the Get Data command button.

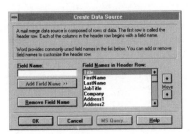

3 When Word displays a list box of data source options, select the Create Data Source entry. Word displays the Create Data Source dialog box.

4 Remove fields you don't need from the Field Names in Header Row list box by selecting them and then selecting the Remove Field Name command button.

5 Add fields you do need but that aren't already in the Field Names in Header Row list box by entering a field name in the Field Name text box and then selecting Add Field Name.

6 Select OK. Word displays the Save Data Source dialog box. Use it to give a name to the database file. (Word database files are simply document files with tables.)

Mailing lists

Word assumes that you want to build a mailing list database, and it lists fields appropriate for such a database. The fields, by the way, are simply the individual chunks of information that are stored for each entry, or record, in the database. In a database that lists names and addresses, each person's name and address represents a record. The fields, or information chunks, might include the person's title, first name, middle initial, last name, street address, city, and state.

continues

Mail Merge *(continued)*

7 Name the file and select a location. (This works the same way as naming a regular document file and selecting its location.)

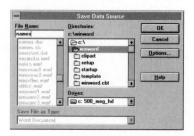

8 When Word asks if you want to add records to the database, indicate that you do by selecting the Edit Data Source command button. Word displays the Data Form dialog box.

9 Enter records into your database by filling in the text boxes and selecting Add New. Use the Record box to move backward and forward in the database. If you enter a record by mistake, display it and select Delete. If you enter some bit of information wrong, display the record, fix the mistake, and move to the next record. When you finish with this step, select OK.

Using an External Database for Mail Merges

You don't have to create a database from scratch if one already exists. Follow these steps to use an existing external database.

1 Choose the Tools Mail Merge command. Word displays the Mail Merge Helper dialog box.

2 Select the Get Data command button.

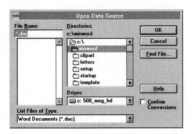

3 When Word displays a list box of data source options, select the Open Data Source entry. Word displays the Open Data Source dialog box.

4 Give the file name and its location. (This works the same way as naming an existing document file and selecting its location.) Then select OK.

Using different file types

Note that you may need to give the file extension if it's something other than DOC. If you want to open a Microsoft Excel database, which is actually called a list, you need to indicate the XLS file extension. You can activate the List Files of Type drop-down list box to see a list of the file formats you can use as data sources.

Describing and Writing the Main Mail Merge Document

Once you've created the main mail merge document and either created or opened the data source, you're ready to specify how the main mail merge document should look.

To create the body text, simply type it in. You should already know how this works. If you're noodling around with Mail Merge, you probably know a thing or two about creating documents.

The only unique feature of using a mail merge document is that you need to tell Word where the database record's fields should get placed. For example, if you've stored a person's title and last name in the database, you may want a form letter's salutation to begin with something along the lines of "Dear Dr. Jekyll" or "Greetings Mr. Hyde."

continues

Mail Merge *(continued)*

To place a database record field into the document, position the insertion point, select the Insert Merge Field tool so that Word displays a list of the database record fields, and select the field.

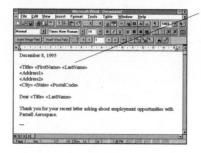

Word adds a field, which simply names the database record field, to the document, as shown in the following example.

Running a Mail Merge

Once you've created the mail merge document, created or opened a data source, and described how the mail merge document should look, you're ready to run the merge. To do this, follow these steps:

1 Choose the Tools Mail Merge command and select the Merge command button. Word displays the Merge dialog box.

2 Use the Merge To drop-down list box to indicate whether Word should create a new document or should simply send stuff to the printer.

3 Select Merge and then stand back. Word runs the mail merge and creates or prints the documents you described.

Margins

The page margins control how much white space appears around the edges of your page. By declaring a border of page space essentially "off-limits," you control how much "printable" space remains.

Changing Page Margins

Choose the File Page Setup command and select the Margins tab to display a dialog box you'll use to specify page margins for printed documents.

1 Use the Top, Bottom, Left, and Right boxes to specify the margin in inches. If you want to specify a gutter, use the Gutter box.

2 Use the Header box to specify how many inches a header should be from the top of the page. Use the Footer box to specify how many inches a footer should be from the bottom of the page.

3 Use the Apply To drop-down list box to specify whether the margin change should apply to the entire document or only from the location of the insertion point forward. If text is selected, the first choice is "Selected Text."

4 Mark the Mirror Margins check box if you will print on both sides of each page of paper and, so, want the margins of facing pages to mirror each other.

 Printing

About gutters

A gutter is simply an extra margin along the edge of the page that is bound. You add gutter margins so that the binding doesn't hide part of the printed document or make the visible page margins look unbalanced.

Master Document A master document is a document that combines other documents, called subdocuments, into one document. I don't cover master documents in this field guide. For more information, see your Word user documentation.

Microsoft Excel You can use Microsoft Excel worksheets and charts in your Word documents.

Select the worksheet range or chart and choose the Edit Copy command. Then switch to the Word application, position the insertion point at the location where you want the worksheet or chart, and choose the Edit Paste command.

🐾 **Object Linking and Embedding; Switching Tasks**

Moving Pictures You can easily move drawing objects and pictures with the mouse. Simply select the object or picture and then drag it to wherever you want it.

Word adds selection handles to the object or picture to show you've selected it. The selection handles are the little black squares appearing at the corners and along each edge.

Another method for moving

You can also move a graphic object or a picture using the Edit Cut and Edit Paste commands in the same way you move other types of data.

🐾 **Frames**

Moving Text

You can move text using either drag-and-drop or the Edit Cut and Edit Paste commands.

Refer to the **Drag-and-Drop** entry if you want to use the mouse and a few deft clicks to move.

If you want to use the Edit Cut and Edit Paste commands—maybe you're someone who doesn't like rodents—follow these steps.

1 Select what you want to move.

2 Choose Edit Cut.

3 Position the insertion point where you want to move whatever it is you're moving.

4 Choose Edit Paste.

⁖ Clipboard; Copying Text

Navigation Keys Your keyboard navigation keys can be a quick and precise way to reposition the **insertion point.** Here are a few of them:

Key or key combination	Where it moves the insertion point
Direction keys	One character or one line in the direction of the arrow
Ctrl + ←	Previous word
Ctrl + →	Next word
Ctrl +↑	Previous paragraph
Ctrl + ↓	Next paragraph
Home	Start of line
End	End of line
Ctrl + PageUp	First character visible in document window
Ctrl + PageDown	Last character visible in document window
PageUp and PageDown	Previous page or next page
Ctrl + Home	First character in document
Ctrl + End	Last character in document

Nonbreaking Spaces Word **word wraps** your lines of text. When you get to the end of a line—say you're in the middle of typing a long word such as Madagascar—Word moves the big word to the next line where there's ample room. Word figures it's fine with you if it breaks your lines of text between words, where there are spaces. Usually, Word is right.

You can, however, use something called a nonbreaking space if you don't want Word to break between two words. To do this, hold down the Ctrl and Shift keys while you press the spacebar. Word places a space in the document—just as if you had pressed only the spacebar—but Word won't break the line at this space. It'll use one of the other spaces in the line.

Nonprinting Characters

Most of what you type into a Word document gets printed. If you think about it for a minute or so, though, you'll realize that not everything you enter prints. Consider, for example, the case of the Enter key. There is no Enter character. When you press Enter, what you've really done is tell Word that a **paragraph** ends at the current **insertion point** location.

Although you may not see anything in the document that shows the end of paragraph, Word places a special character in the document that basically says, "Uh-oh. The user wants the paragraph to end here. I better remember this." Word also places other characters into a document for other keys you type but Word doesn't print—tabs and spaces being the most common.

To see these nonprinting characters, choose the Tools Options command, select the View page tab, and then mark the Nonprinting Characters check boxes.

Chapter·13·-·Smorgasbord¶
¶
→ I·squatted·in·the·tall·grass·and·tried·not·to·move.·Foolishly,·I·thought,·the·lion·might·choose·some·other·entrées·for·lunch.·Would·not·a·fleet-footed·antelope·be·more·sporting?¶

An end-of-paragraph character. You enter this by pressing Enter.

A space character. You enter this by pressing the spacebar. But you already knew this, right?

A tab character. I feel stupid telling you this, but parallel structure and a compulsive personality require me to tell you that you enter this by pressing Tab. Sorry.

Numbered Lists

You can create numbered lists of paragraphs. (Each paragraph is considered a list entry.)

Creating a Numbered List

To create a numbered list, select the **paragraphs** you want in the list. Then choose the Format Bullets and Numbering command and select the Numbered page tab.

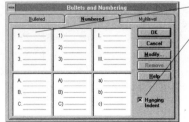

Click on one of the numbered list examples.

Use the Hanging Indent check box to specify if the second and subsequent lines of the paragraph or only the first line should be indented.

Adding Numbered List Entries

To add an entry to a numbered list, place the insertion point at the end of an existing entry, press Enter, and then type the new list entry.

Removing Numbered List Entries

To remove an entry from a numbered list, select it and press Del.

 Bulleted Lists

Automatic renumbering

Word automatically renumbers the items in a numbered list as you add and remove items.

Object Linking and Embedding
Object linking and embedding, or OLE, is a Windows feature.

What OLE Does

You use it to create what's called a compound document—a document file that combines two or more types of documents. For example, you might want to create a compound document that includes a long report written in, for example, Word for Windows. On page 27 of your report, however, you might want to include a worksheet (or worksheet fragment) created in Excel. And perhaps on page 37 of your report, you might want to include a chart created in Excel. So your compound document really consists of stuff created in different applications and pasted together into one big, compound document.

Using OLE to Create Compound Documents

To do all this pasting together and combining, you can often use the application's Edit Copy and Edit Paste (or Edit Paste Special) commands. And if you're creating the compound document in Word, you can use the Insert Object command.

Distinguishing Between Linked Objects and Embedded Objects

A linked object—remember this might be the Excel worksheet you've pasted into a Word document—gets updated whenever the source document changes. An embedded object doesn't. (You can, however, double-click an embedded object to open the application that created the embedded object to make your changes.)

Embedding and Linking Existing Objects; Embedding New Objects

What you absolutely need to know about OLE

Perhaps the most important tidbit for you to know about OLE is that it's very easy to use. You don't have to do anything other than copy and paste the things—called objects—you want to plop into the compound document.

Opening Documents To open a previously saved document, choose the File Open command.

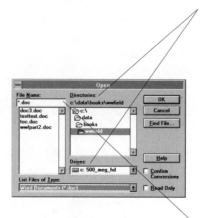

1 Use the Directories and Drives list boxes to specify where the document file was saved.

2 Use the List Files of Type list box if you want to open a file with a format other than that of the usual Word document file. (You might do this if you want to import another word-processing program's file.)

3 Use the File Name text box or the File Name list box to identify the file.

4 If you don't want to overwrite the original document file, mark the Read Only check box. If you mark this check box and later you want to save the document, you'll need to use a new file name.

5 Select OK.

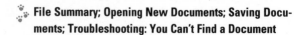

🐾 **File Summary; Opening New Documents; Saving Documents; Troubleshooting: You Can't Find a Document**

Numbered File menu commands

Microsoft Word provides numbered File menu commands for opening the last four documents you saved. With a couple of clicks, you can open one of these documents.

Opening New Documents To create a new document, select the File New command or select the New tool.

If you choose the File New command, Word displays the New dialog box. Select a document template that uses formatting close to the formatting you want your new document to use. Or, if you don't know what formatting you want your new document to use, select the Normal template. Then select OK. You're done.

❖ **Opening Documents; Templates; Wizards**

Orphan In printed documents, an orphan occurs when the first line of a **paragraph** prints on one page and the rest of the paragraph prints on the next page. Using the Format Paragraph command's **Text Flow** tab options, you can tell Word to eliminate orphans by always breaking a paragraph so that at least the first 2 lines of a paragraph get printed on a page.

❖ **Widow**

Outlining Whether you're writing a novel, a term paper, an annual report—actually, any document longer than a few paragraphs—the first step is to create an outline. Yeah, I know—you really, really don't want to do this, even though you also know you should.

Well, Word makes it easy. With Word, it's easy to create an outline, and it's easy to change it—condense it, expand it, totally revise it, whatever.

First you provide headings for each part of your document—for example, the titles of the chapters of a book. Then you provide subheadings for each of the headings. If necessary, you continue this process by providing sub-subheadings for each of the subheadings.

continues

Outlining *(continued)*

The next figure shows an early version of the outline for *Microsoft Excel Field Guide,* another title in the Field Guide series.

> ✧ **I. Environment**
>   ▫ *A. Excel Application Window*
>   ▫ *B. Creating a Worksheet*
>   ▫ *C. Charting*
>   ▫ *D. Creating a List*
> ▫ **Part II. Field Guide**
> ▫ **Part III. Trouble-shooting**
> ▫ **Part IV. Quick Reference**
> ▬

Creating an Outline

To create an outline, follow these steps:

1 Create a new **document** based on the Normal document **template** by choosing the File New command and pressing Enter.

2 Choose the View Outline command. Word adds the outlining **toolbar** to the **application window**.

3 Enter the lines of text that describe each major and minor part within the document. (Each line of text should be entered as a **paragraph**.)

4 Indent the parts within a part by selecting the part you want to indent and then choosing the Demote toolbar button.

Using the Outlining Toolbar Buttons

The outlining toolbar provides a series of buttons useful for creating and revising outlines. Note that because you end an outline level by pressing Enter, each outline level is actually a paragraph.

Tool	What it does
⬅	Promotes selected paragraph to next, higher outline level
➡	Demotes selected paragraph to next, lower outline level
⏩	Demotes selected paragraph to the lowest outline level, which is document body text
⬆	Moves the selected paragraph so that it's in front of the preceding paragraph
⬇	Moves the selected paragraph so that it's behind the following paragraph
➕	Displays the next, lower outline level if it's previously been hidden
➖	Hides the next, lower outline level
1	Displays all the heading 1 levels in the outline
2	Displays all the heading 1 and 2 levels in the outline
3	Displays all the heading 1-3 levels in the outline
4	Displays all the heading 1-4 levels in the outline
5	Displays all the heading 1-5 levels in the outline
6	Displays all the heading 1-6 levels in the outline
7	Displays all the heading 1-7 levels in the outline
8	Displays all the heading 1-8 levels in the outline

continues

Outlining *(continued)*

All	Displays all the heading levels in the outline
	Displays only the first line of paragraph of body text
	Toggles the displayed—but not the printed—formatting of all characters between formatted and unformatted
	Displays master document view

Beginning Your Writing

To begin your writing, choose the View Normal or View Page Layout command. Word uses the parts, subparts, and sub-subparts you entered to create the outline as headings in the document. You simply enter paragraphs that follow each heading.

Tables of contents and outlines

One other advantage of Word's outlining feature is that when you use it you can generate a table of contents almost automatically. To do this, choose the Insert Index and Tables command; then select the Table of Contents tab and OK.

Page Breaks   Page breaks are the points where the document is split between pages.

Automatic Page Breaks

Word automatically adds page breaks as you create your document. Automatic page breaks appear in the document as dotted lines.

Manual, or Hard, Page Breaks

You can add a manual, or hard, page break. To do so, position the **insertion point** at the point—usually the start of a line—the page break should precede, choose the Insert Break command, and then mark the Page Break radio button. Word identifies page breaks you've added this way by placing the word "Page Break" in the dotted, page-break line.

Removing page breaks

You can remove hard page breaks. To do so, select
the page break and then press Del.

Page Numbers You can number your document pages. To do
this, choose the Insert Page Numbers command.

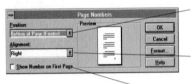

Use the Position drop-
down list box to place
the page numbers.

Use the Alignment box to
specify how page num-
bers should be aligned.

Use this option to indi-
cate whether the first
page should have a
printed page number.

Where page numbers go

Page numbers appear in either the header or the footer. In effect, when you insert page numbers, you add a header or a footer that shows the page number.

Page Orientation The orientation of a page is either vertical
(portrait) or horizontal (landscape). To select page
orientation, choose the File Page Setup command, select
the Paper Size tab, and then mark either the Portrait or
Landscape button. If you're not sure which orientation
you want, simply look at the Preview box. It shows how
the printed page changes as you click the Orientation
buttons.

Page Tab If a dialog box contains more options than will fit within its border, the dialog box uses several pages. Each page displays a related set of needed input information. You can move through these pages by clicking on the page tabs. To see an example of how this works, choose the File Page Setup command and then alternately click the Page, Margins, Paper Size, Paper Source, and Layout tabs. I'm not going to include a figure that shows this. I don't want to ruin the surprise for you.

Pagination Pagination refers to the process of breaking a document into page-sized chunks. You can let Word paginate your documents. Or you can do it yourself using hard page breaks. Know, however, that Word usually does a pretty good job.

🐾 **Page Breaks**

Paragraph Borders You can add border lines to paragraphs.
To do so, follow these steps:

1 Select the paragraph.

2 Choose the Format Borders and Shading command. Word displays
the Paragraph Borders and Shading dialog box.

3 Select the Borders tab. Word displays the border options.

4 Use the Presets buttons to choose either the box border or the box
with shadow border. The Border box shows the position and layout of your border choice.

5 Use the From Text box to indicate how much white space should
separate the border and the paragraph. One point is 1/72 inch.

6 Use the Line, Style, and Color lists to select a border line thickness
and a color (if you want something besides basic black).

Paragraph and Line Spacing
Remember that each time you press Enter, you signal to Word that you've ended a paragraph. If you want to add lines in front of or after these paragraphs, you can use the Format Paragraph command.

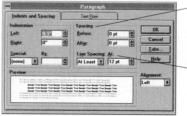

Use the Before and After boxes to specify the paragraph spacing in points.

Use the Line Spacing and At boxes to specify the line spacing.

Paragraphs
In prose, a paragraph is a group of sentences. Ideally, it starts with a topic sentence and develops a single thought. High school composition, so I hear, was a breeze if you could write solid, well-structured paragraphs.

In Word, a paragraph is simply a chunk of text that ends where you press Enter. So you can have a paragraph that's a single character, a sentence, or a group of sentences. All you have to do is press Enter.

This may all seem like much ado about nothing, but you should remember what paragraphs are—at least from Word's point of view. The reason is that much of the **formatting** you do in Word applies to paragraphs. You can, for example, format paragraphs by changing indenting, line spacing, and alignment. And you can also control the way **pagination** affects your paragraph.

> **Indenting and Alignment; Paragraph and Line Spacing; Widow**

Passwords
You can use passwords to limit access to a file and to limit changes to a document. How you do both of these things is described elsewhere in this book.

> **Protecting Documents; Save Options**

Points One point equals 1/72 inch. In Word, you specify font size and row heights in points. You can also specify most other vertical measurements in points by entering the number of points and then the letter "p."

⁘ **Changing Fonts**

Printing To print the **document** displayed in the **document window,** choose the File Print command. Or click the Print tool. If you choose the File Print command, Word displays the Print dialog box. Use it to specify how Word should print, and then select OK.

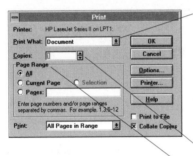

Use the Print What drop-down list box to indicate whether you want to print the document—the usual choice—or something else related to the document such as the file summary information or the styles list.

You can guess what the Copies box does, right?

If you want, you can print some portion of the document, for example pages 2-8, using the Page Range options.

⁘ **Print Preview**

Print Preview Choose the File Print Preview command when you want to see how a document's pages will look. When you choose the command, Word displays a reduced image of the page in the middle of the **application window**. Use the PageUp and PageDown keys to move through the **document**. Click on the document to alternately enlarge or reduce the displayed page size. To turn off the Print Preview display, choose Close.

❖ **Printing**

Protecting Documents Choose the Tools Protect Document command to prevent or minimize changes to a **document**.

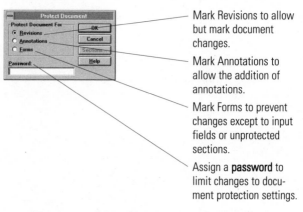

Mark Revisions to allow but mark document changes.

Mark Annotations to allow the addition of annotations.

Mark Forms to prevent changes except to input fields or unprotected sections.

Assign a **password** to limit changes to document protection settings.

❖ **Annotations; Revision Marks; Save Options**

About passwords

You can use as many as 15 characters in a password. Word accepts letters, numbers, symbols, and spaces.

Readability Word measures the readability of your **document** when it checks grammar.

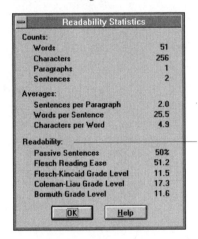

Readability Statistics	
Counts:	
Words	51
Characters	256
Paragraphs	1
Sentences	2
Averages:	
Sentences per Paragraph	2.0
Words per Sentence	25.5
Characters per Word	4.9
Readability:	
Passive Sentences	50%
Flesch Reading Ease	51.2
Flesch-Kincaid Grade Level	11.5
Coleman-Liau Grade Level	17.3
Bormuth Grade Level	11.6

Word calculates several measures of readability.

 Grammar Checking

Repeat Don't worry. I'm not about to launch into that annoying little joke "Pete and Repeat." (Pete and Repeat want to cross the river, but the boat only holds one person. So Pete crosses first. Who's left?) I just thought I would point out that you can usually repeat your last change to a document by choosing the Edit Repeat command.

Replacing Text Choose the Edit Replace command to locate and replace text. To use the Edit Replace command, follow these steps:

1 Select the document area Word should search if you want to limit the replacement. If you don't select an area, Word searches through the entire document and gives you the option of replacing text throughout the document.

2 Choose the Edit Replace command.

3 Use the Find What text box to specify what you want to replace.

4 Use the Replace With text box to specify the replacement text.

5 Use the Search drop-down list box to indicate whether Word should search Down (from the insertion point to the end of the document), Up (from the insertion point to the beginning of the document), or All (the entire document).

6 Use the Match Case and Find Whole Words Only check boxes to indicate whether Word should consider case (lower vs. upper) in its search and look for whole words rather than partial words.

7 Select Find Next to start and restart the search.

8 Select Replace to substitute the replacement text.

9 Select Replace All to substitute the replacement text without your intervention.

 Finding Text

Replacing formatting

Usually, you'll use the Edit Replace command to replace text. You can also use it to replace formatting. To do this, move the insertion point to the Find What text box, select the Format command button, select a type of formatting from the list Word displays, and then describe the formatting you're looking for. Then move the insertion point to the Replace With text box, select the Format button, select a formatting type, and then describe the replacement formatting.

Resizing Pictures Use the mouse to resize pictures. To do this, select the object or picture. Word marks the picture with selection handles. (The selection handles, as you may already know, are those little black squares.) To change the picture's size, drag the selection handles.

⁘ Adding Document Pictures; Moving Pictures

Revision Marks You can tell Word to keep track of the changes you make (or someone else makes) to a document.

Adding Revision Marks

Choose the Tools Revisions command.

Use the check boxes to tell Word how and where it should show revisions.

Word draws bars in the margins to flag lines with changed text, crosses out deleted text, and underlines new text.

continues

Revision Marks *(continued)*

Accepting Revisions

Choose the Tools Revisions command and select the Accept All command button to update the document so that it includes the revisions. Word also removes the revision marks when you do this.

Rejecting Revisions

Select the Reject All command button to undo the revisions. Or you can select the Review command button to selectively review and then accept or reject each revision.

Exporting documents with revision marks

You'll find it's cleanest to export documents that don't have revision marks. For example, even when moving documents between Microsoft Word for the Apple Macintosh and Microsoft Word for Windows, the revision marks, crossed-out text, and added text often seem to get goofed up.

Right-Justify

You can right-justify text by telling Word you want to use justified alignment. In this case, each line of text starts at the left margin and ends at the right margin. To do this, select the paragraphs you want to justify. Then select the Justify button on the Formatting toolbar.

❖ **Indenting and Alignment**

Ruler

The ruler appears below the **toolbars**.

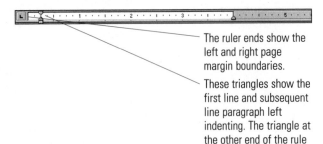

The ruler ends show the left and right page margin boundaries.

These triangles show the first line and subsequent line paragraph left indenting. The triangle at the other end of the rule shows right indenting.

Indenting and Alignment; Margins

Changing indents and margins with the ruler

Drag the ruler's indent triangles and margin boundaries to change indents and margins.

Save Options

The Tools Options command provides a Save tab, which lets you protect document files from accidental deletion and from people who don't have a **password** to view them. I won't describe all these options—only the handful that are most helpful.

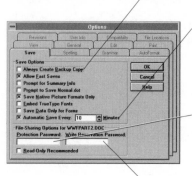

Mark the Always Create Backup Copy check box to create a duplicate copy of the document whenever you save the document.

If you want Word to save the document periodically, use these options to tell Word it should automatically save and how often.

You can limit viewing of the file by assigning a protection password. Word asks for the protection password when someone attempts to open the document using the File Open command.

Limit changes to the file by assigning a write reservation password. Word asks for the write reservation password when someone attempts to save the document using the File Save command. (Note, however, that even with a write reservation password, someone can still save a copy of the document with a new name.)

⁂ **File Summary; Saving Documents**

Saving Documents

 To save documents, you use either the File Save or the File Save As command or the Save tool. Which command you use depends on whether you've already saved the document.

Saving a Document You've Already Saved

Choose the File Save command or the Save tool. This tells Word to save the active file using the same name and in the same location.

Saving a Document for the First Time

To save a document for the first time, follow these steps:

1 Choose the File Save As command or the Save tool.

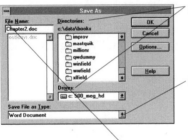

2 Use the Directories and Drives list boxes to specify where the document should be placed.

3 Use the Save File As Type list box to save the file in a format other than the usual, Word document format file. (Do this, for example, to use the file with another word-processor.)

4 Use the File Name text box to name the file, but don't enter the file extension. Word adds this for you because it uses the extension to identify the file type.

⋮ **File Names; File Summary; Opening Documents; Save Options**

Saving Documents *(continued)*

Renaming documents

Choose the File Save As command when you want to save a document with a new name or in a new location.

Scrolling Scrolling simply refers to paging through a **document**. You can use the vertical scroll bars if you've got a mouse. You can use the PageUp and PageDown keys—or one of the other **navigation keys** or key combinations. Or you can use the Edit **Go To** command.

Sections You can break Word documents into parts called "sections." To do this, choose the Insert Break command. (When you choose the command, you mark one of the radio buttons that indicates you want a section break.)

Sections can seem kind of funny. Actually, I think section breaks are most useful for headers and footers. If you set up a header or a footer for a file, it will apply to every page unless there is a section break—then you can change it. Some people use sections to lay out pages differently— for example, by using different margins.

Selecting When you want to move, copy, delete, or format some element of a Word document, you need to first select it. The easiest way to do this is by clicking and sometimes dragging the mouse. (In fact, if you don't have a mouse, your next best investment in computer hardware is a mouse.)

Selecting Words

Select words by double-clicking them with the mouse.

Selecting Line Fragments

Select chunks of text—including single characters—by clicking in front of the first character and then dragging the mouse to just following the last character. Word flips the colors of selected text—black becomes white and white becomes black—to highlight your selection.

Selecting Sentences

Select a sentence by pressing Ctrl and clicking the sentence.

Selecting a Single Line of Text

Select lines of text by clicking in the selection bar (the area directly to the left of text) adjacent to the line.

Selecting Multiple Lines of Text

Select multiple lines of text by clicking the selection bar and dragging the mouse. (Try this if you have questions. It's very straightforward.)

Selecting Paragraphs

You can select an entire paragraph by double-clicking the selection bar next to the paragraph. Or you can triple-click a word in the paragraph.

Selecting Objects and Pictures

Select objects and pictures by clicking on them. Click any place. It doesn't matter where. Objects and pictures show selection handles (little black squares on their corners and sides).

When in doubt about how to select

If you don't know how to select something, try clicking on it. Or try dragging the mouse over it.

Shortcut Menus

Word knows which commands make sense in which situations. It also knows which commands you, as a Word user, are most likely to use. If you want it to, Word will display a menu of these commands—called the shortcut menu. All you need to do is click the right button on the mouse. (Remember that you use the left mouse button for selecting menus, commands, dialog box elements, and assorted and sundry items.)

Sorting

You can sort **paragraphs** and **table** rows using the Table Sort command.

Sorting Paragraphs

To sort paragraphs, select them and then choose the Table Sort Text command.

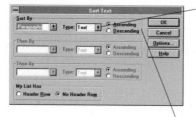

Tell Word how paragraphs should be sorted. Text means alphabetically by the letters that start the paragraph. You can also sort the paragraph using a date or a number if these are the pieces of data that start the paragraphs.

Tell Word whether paragraphs should be organized in A to Z (ascending) or Z to A (descending) order.

A friendly reminder

Remember, a paragraph in Word is simply a chunk of text that you end by pressing Enter.

Sorting Table Rows

Sorting table rows can get a bit more complicated. You need to follow these steps:

1 Select the table.

2 Choose the Table Sort command.

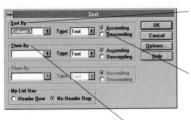

3 Use the Sort By drop-down list box to name the row you use for alphabetizing or ordering.

4 Use the Sort By radio buttons to indicate whether you want alphabetic list entries arranged in A to Z (ascending) or Z to A (descending) order.

5 Use the Then By drop-down list boxes and radio button sets to add second and third items that Word will sort by if the first items are equal.

6 Use the My List Has radio buttons to indicate whether the first selected row is a header that shouldn't be sorted.

Spelling You can use the Tools Spelling command to check the spelling of words in your document. To use the command, select the document portion you want to spell-check (if you're interested in checking only a limited area); then choose the command. If Word finds no misspelled words, it displays a message box that simply tells you it's checked the words in your selection. If Word does finds a mispelled word, it displays the Spelling dialog box. Use it to control how Word spell-checks and what Word does when it finds a possible error.

continues

Spelling *(continued)*

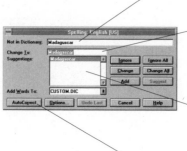

Word alerts you to words it can't find in its dictionary with the Not in Dictionary text box.

Word suggests an alternative spelling in the Change To text box. But you can edit whatever Word suggests.

Other words that are spelled similarly to what you entered may appear in the Suggestions list box. You can select any of these by clicking.

Is this a word you often misspell? You can add the misspelled word/correctly spelled word combination to AutoCorrect's list of common mistakes.

Spelling Command Buttons

Once Word finds a potentially misspelled word, you use the Spelling command buttons to indicate what Word should do:

Button	What it does
Ignore	Ignores only this occurrence of the word
Ignore All	Ignores this and every other occurrence of the word
Change	Changes this occurrence of the word to what the Change To text box shows
Change All	Changes this and every other occurrence of the word to what the Change To text box shows
Add	Adds the word to the spelling dictionary named in the Add Words To drop-down list box
Suggest	Looks through the Word spelling dictionary and the custom dictionary named in the Add Words To drop-down list box for similarly spelled words

AutoCorrect

If Word can't find your word

You can use the wildcard characters ? and * in the Change To box to find words spelled similarly to what you enter. You can use the * character to represent any combination of characters, and you can use the ? character to represent any single character. For example, if you're trying to spell the word that starts with the letters "Colo" but you don't know which letters follow—and Word doesn't either—type Colo* in the Change To text box; then select Suggest. Word will find all the words in its dictionary that start with the letters "Colo."

Splitting Documents

If a document gets too big for its own good, you can split it into two or more smaller documents. Before you do this, however, save the big document—just to be safe. Then follow these steps:

1 Select a chunk of existing document that you want to move to a new document.

2 Select the Cut tool to move the current document selection to the Clipboard.

3 Open a new document—for example, by choosing the New tool.

4 Choose the Paste tool so that the Clipboard contents are pasted into the new document.

5 Save the new document. (It now contains only what you cut and pasted from the original document.)

6 Save the original document. (It now contains only what remains after you cut and pasted portions to the new document.)

⁙ **Clipboard; Opening New Documents; Saving Documents**

Using a master document

There's another way to make documents more manageable. You can create a master document that uses subdocuments as its sections. I don't think many casual users will want to get this sophisticated. So I won't describe how the whole master-document thing works. Be aware, however, that the feature exists. You can find information on master documents in you Word user documentation.

Starting Word
You start Word the same way you start any Windows application.

Starting Word Manually

To start Word manually, follow these steps:

1 Start Windows—for example, by typing *win* at the MS-DOS prompt.

2 Display the program group in which Word is an item. For example, if Word's program group is Microsoft Office—and it probably is—choose the Window Microsoft Office command from the Program Manager menu bar.

3 Double-click on the Microsoft Word program item.

Starting Word Automatically

To start Word each time Windows starts, follow these steps:

1 Start Windows—for example, by typing *win* at the MS-DOS prompt.

2 Display the program group in which Word is an item. For example, if Word's program group is Microsoft Office —and it probably is—choose the Window Microsoft Office command from the Program Manager menu bar.

3 Display the Startup program group—for example, by choosing the Window Startup command from the Program Manager menu bar.

4 Drag the Microsoft Word program item icon from the Microsoft Office program group window to the Startup program group window.

Styles
Styles combine **font**, **paragraph**, **tab**, **border**, **frame**, language, and numbered list formats. You use styles so that you can simultaneously apply a combination of formatting changes to a document selection and so that you can easily change formatting throughout a **document**. One other tidbit you may find helpful to know is this: For the most part, document **templates** are collections of styles.

⁙ **Applying Styles; Changing Styles; Creating Styles**

Switching Tasks To multitask, or run multiple applications, in the Windows operating environment, you use the Control menu's Switch To command. Selecting this command displays the Task List dialog box, which works as described below:

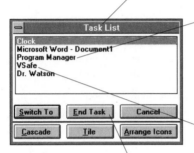

The Task List dialog box lists the Program Manager, as well as any other applications that you or Windows has started.

To start a new application, double-click the Program Manager. Then, when Windows displays the Program Manager, use it to start another application.

To switch to an application already running, double-click it. Or select it with the direction keys or the mouse, and choose Switch To.

Use the Cascade, Tile, and Arrange Icons command buttons to manage the application windows of the applications you've started.

You can use the End Task command button as a last resort to terminate a Windows application you can't stop any other way.

Easy switching

You can cycle through the applications listed in the Task List dialog box by pressing Alt+Tab.

Symbols

You can use symbols in a document even if you don't see a character key on your keyboard for the symbol. Let's say, for example, that you want to use the skull and crossbones symbol:

I won't ask why you're using this character. It's not really any of my business. Who knows? Maybe you're writing an article about pirates.

Adding Symbols

To add symbols to a document, follow these steps:

1 Move the insertion point to the place where you want the symbol.

2 Choose the Insert Symbol command.

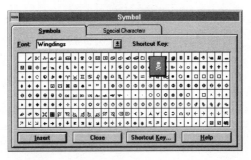

3 Select the Symbols tab if you want to use a symbol from one of the font character sets—such as one of the TrueType font sets.

4 Use the Font drop-down list box to specify which font you want. To add a skull and crossbones character to a document, you would specify Wingdings. Once you specify the font set, Word displays a grid of the characters. Word magnifies the selected character.

5 Select the character by clicking the mouse. It's a little difficult to see the Wingding characters in detail, so you may need to squint your eyes, or failing that, experiment a bit by selecting a character to magnify it and then using the direction keys to see others.

6 Select Insert to add the symbol to your document.

Deleting Symbols

Symbols are characters. To delete a symbol, select it and press Del. Or backspace over the symbol.

 Fonts

Typesetting characters

Select the Special Characters tab to display a list of typesetting characters such a the en dash, the em dash, and the copyright symbol. Word displays a short list box from which you can select one of these characters.

Adding ANSI Characters

The ANSI character set includes all the ASCII characters your keyboard shows plus the special characters your keyboard doesn't show, such as the Japanese yen symbol, ¥, or the British pound, £. Even though these special characters don't appear on your keyboard and may not be symbol characters, you can still use them in Word documents.

To insert an ANSI character in a document, position the insertion point where you want the character, hold down Alt, and then, using the numeric keyboard, enter the ANSI code for that character. For example, the ANSI character code for the Japanese yen symbol is 0165. To enter a yen symbol into a document, hold down Alt and type 0165 using the numeric keypad. (You can get ANSI character codes from the Windows user guide.)

Removing ANSI Characters

To delete an ANSI character, select it and press Del, or backspace over the character.

Synonyms
A synonym is a word that has the same meaning as another word. Hot and fiery. Cold and icy. You get the idea, right? Use the **Thesaurus** to find a synonym.

 Antonyms

Table Alignment To change the way a table aligns against a page's margins, select the table and choose the Table Cell Height and Width command. Then mark one of the alignment radio buttons: Left, Center, or Right.

Table AutoFormats You can have Word format the selected table. To do this, select the table and choose the Table Table AutoFormat command.

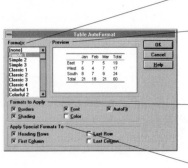

Select a format from the Formats list box.

Look at the Preview box to see how your formatting looks when applied to a sample table.

Use the Formats to Apply check boxes to add or re-move elements of the automatic formatting.

Use the Apply Special Formats To check boxes to remove formatting from specified columns and rows.

Table Borders You can add border lines to tables and to the column and row edges of tables. To do so, follow these steps:

1 Select the table.

2 Choose the Format Borders and Shading command. Word displays the Table Borders and Shading dialog box.

3 Select the Borders tab. Word displays the border options.

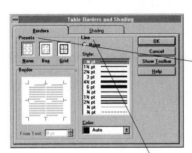

4 Use the Presets buttons to choose either the Box border or the Grid border. Box draws a border around the table edge. Grid draws a border around the table edge and between the columns and rows. The Border box shows the position and layout of your border choice.

5 Use the Line, Style, and Color lists to select a border line thickness and a color (if you want something besides basic black).

Table Columns You can change the width of table columns easily and quickly. Simply select the column (such as by clicking on the column and choosing the Table Select Column command); then drag the column's right edge to change its width.

If you don't like to use the mouse, you can also select the column and then use the Table Cell Height and Width command.

⁛ Table Rows; Tables

Table Headings If a table gets broken across pages, you can tell Word to repeat the table's headings on the second and subsequent pages. To do this, select the row or rows that show the table headings and then choose the Table Headings command. This command is a toggle switch—it turns on and off the table headings feature. So, to later remove the table headings, choose the command again.

Table Rows You can change the height of table rows. To do this, follow these steps:

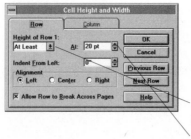

1 Select the row.

2 Choose the Table Cell Height and Width command.

3 Select the Row page tab.

4 Select the At Least entry.

5 Enter the row height in **points**.

⁛ Table Columns; Tables

Tables Tables use columns and rows to arrange information. They've been around for years. Henry David Thoreau, for example, summarized the construction costs of his cabin at Walden Pond with a table.

⁝ Creating Tables; Formulas

Tables of Contents A table of contents lists the parts that make up a document and gives the page numbers on which the parts start. In a novel, for example, the table of contents lists the chapters and gives the page numbers on which the chapters start.

Creating Tables of Contents Based on Outlines

If you used Word's outlining feature, you can create a table of contents by choosing the Insert Index and Tables command, selecting the Table of Contents page tab (so that Word displays the Table of Contents options), and selecting OK. Selecting OK accepts Word's suggestions for table of contents organization and layout. Be sure to place the insertion point where you want the table of contents before telling Word to generate the table.

Customizing a Table of Contents

You can also make changes to what Word suggests using the Table of Contents tab in the Index and Tables dialog box.

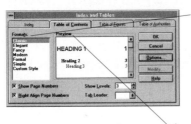

Choose a table of contents style from the Formats list box.

Use the Show Page Numbers and Right Align Page Numbers check boxes to tell Word whether and where you want page numbers.

Use the Preview box to see how your table of contents will look.

continues

Tables of Contents *(continued)*

Creating Tables of Contents If You Didn't Outline

If you didn't use Word's outlining feature, you can still easily build a table of contents as long as you used styles for the document parts you want listed in you table. To do this, choose the Insert Index and Tables command (so Word displays the Index and Tables dialog box), select the Table of Contents tab, and then select the Options command button (so that Word displays the Table of Contents Options dialog box).

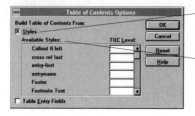

Tell Word you want it to build a table of contents using document styles.

Indicate which styles should be listed in the table of contents by entering the number 1 in the highest level style, the number 2 in the next highest level style, and so on.

Select OK to close the Table of Contents Options dialog box.

Tabs   In the old days, you used the tab key to move your typewriter carriage to the next tab stop. Typically, you did this for two reasons: to indent text—such as the first lines of paragraphs—and to create **tables.** In Word, paragraph indenting is a formatting choice. (This saves you from having to press Tab.) And tables are created using the Table menu commands.

Dare I say next what I'm thinking and what you're wondering? I shall. Tabs are, for most Word users, obsolete. There are better and easier ways to indent. There are easier and better ways to create tables.

🐾 **Indenting and Alignment**

Templates A template is a collection of formatting styles; **AutoText** entries; **macros** (if you've created these); and menu, shortcut, and toolbar changes (if you've made these.)

When you start Word, it uses a template named NORMAL.DOT to create a blank document. But, by choosing the File New command to create new documents, you can create a document based on some other tailored set of formatting styles. Word, for example, supplies an Invoice template that is all set up for creating invoices. (This template includes formulas that calculate your invoice subtotals and grand total, for example.) Word also supplies templates for fax covers, letters, press releases, and reports.

⠶ **Formulas; Styles**

Text Flow Text flow refers to how Word breaks **paragraphs** between pages, how it hyphenates, and how it numbers the lines of a **document**.

To control text flow, choose the Format Paragraph command, select the Text Flow page tab, and then mark the appropriate check boxes. You can use the Preview box to see, roughly, how your text flow control settings work.

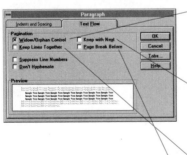

Widow/Orphan Control tells Word not to print the first or last line of a paragraph on a separate page.

Keep with Next tells Word not to page break between the selected paragraph and the next paragraph.

Keep Lines Together tells Word not to page break the selected paragraph.

Page Break Before tells Word to start this paragraph on a new page.

⠶ **Hyphenation; Line Numbers; Orphan; Widow**

Thesaurus Use Word's Thesaurus to find **antonyms** and **synonyms** for the selected word. To use the Thesaurus, select the word for which you want to find an antonym or a synomym. Then choose the Tools Thesaurus command.

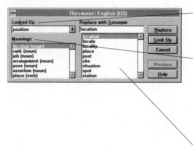

The Looked Up box shows the word you selected.

Select the word meaning you want if you're looking for a synonym. Or scroll to the very end of this list and select Antonyms.

Select the synonym or antonym you want to replace for the selected word from the Replace with list box.

Times You can enter a **field** for the current system time at the **insertion point** by pressing Alt+Shift+T. You can also use the Insert Date and Time command, but mark the Insert as Field check box to make the date a field. Either way, Word enters the time in HH:MM pm/am format. So, if it's 4 o'clock in the afternoon, Word enters 4:00 PM.

 Dates

Tip of the Day When Word starts, it displays a message box with some helpful nugget of knowledge, called the Tip of the Day. You can select OK to continue. You don't have to read the tip.

If you don't read the tip of the day

Unmark the Show Tips at Startup check box if you're not interested in reading the tip of the day.

Toolbars Toolbars are those rows of buttons and boxes that appear at the top of your **application window** just below the menu bar. Word initially displays the Standard toolbar and the Formatting toolbar. But Word also provides several other toolbars. You can add and remove any toolbars by pointing to the toolbar, clicking the right mouse button (instead of the usual left button), and then—when Word displays a list of the available toolbars—selecting the one you want. (You can also use the View Toolbars command to accomplish the same thing.)

Toolbar button names

If you place the mouse pointer over a toolbar button, Word displays the button name in a tiny, yellow box.

TrueType TrueType is Microsoft Corporation's scalable font technology. If you're working with Word, using TrueType fonts in your documents delivers two benefits. First, Word comes with some cool TrueType fonts. (OK. Maybe that shouldn't count as a benefit, but with Word you don't get PostScript, which is the competitive scalable font product.) Second, because of the way a scalable font is created, it's easy for Word to change the point size in a way that results in legible fonts. Word identifies TrueType fonts in the various Font list boxes with the **Tr** prefix.

🐾 **Changing Fonts; Fonts**

Underline Characters You can <u>underline</u> characters by selecting them and then pressing Ctrl+U or clicking the Underline formatting toolbar button. You can also use the Format Font command.

🐾 **Changing Fonts**

Undo You can undo your changes to a document one change at time or in groups. To reverse document changes, a change at a time, choose the Edit Undo command. Or choose the Undo tool.

You can also undo selected changes or a series of changes by activating the Undo list box—click the down arrow right of the Undo button—and then selecting the oldest action you want to undo.

Widow In printed **documents**, a widow occurs when the last line of a **paragraph** is printed on the next page. Using the Format Paragraph command's **Text Flow** tab options, you can tell Word to eliminate widows by always breaking a paragraph so at least the last two lines get printed on the next page.

 Orphan

Window Command Buttons Arranged around the outside edge of the Word **application window** and the **document windows** are command buttons. You can use these command buttons to display the Control menu, to close windows, and to minimize and change window size.

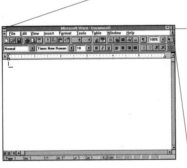

Click these buttons, called the Control-menu boxes, to display a window's Control menu.

Click these buttons to minimize a window so that it appears only as an icon. (Minimized document windows appear as icons at the bottom of the application window.)

The Maximize/Restore buttons' appearance depends on the window's size. If a window isn't maximized, click the button that looks like an upward pointing arrow head to maximize. If a window is maximized, click the button that looks like a double-headed arrow head to restore a window to its usual, unmaximized size.

A quick exit

You can close a document window by double-clicking its Control-menu box. You can also close an application window by double-clicking its Control-menu box.

Window Panes

You can split a document window into panes and then use the panes to view different portions of the same document. You might do this to view a document's **table of contents** from page 1 in one pane and something from the fifth **section** of the document from page 21 in another pane.

Creating Window Panes

Follow these steps to split a window into panes:

1 Choose the Window Split command to split the active document window into two panes. To show the split window, Word draws a fuzzy, thick horizontal line through the middle of the document window.

2 Use the up and down direction keys to move this line to the place you want the window split.

3 Press Enter to anchor the pane line. Word replaces the fuzzy thick line with a second ruler for the new document pane.

Removing Window Panes

To remove a window pane, choose the Window Remove Split command. (This command replaces the Window Split command once you've split a window into panes.)

Jumping between window panes

You can move the **insertion point** between window panes by clicking.

Wizards If you've got a complicated document to create—something like a newsletter, say, or a legal pleading—Word has some extra special tricks up its sleeve for you. When you choose the File New command to create the new document, you can select one of the wizards identified in the template list box. When you do, Word collects information about the document you want to create and uses this data to make a series of document, section, and paragraph formatting changes. You may never need or use this feature, but take a gander at the list that follows. If you need to create any of the following documents, try using one of the Word wizards as a first step:

Wizard	What it does
Agenda	Builds a meeting agenda document
Award	Creates an award and allows you to easily add WordArt objects
Calendar	Draws a calendar table
Letter	Creates a formal business letter document
Fax	Creates a fax cover letter
Memo	Whips up a clever-looking memo you can send to your boss
Newsletter	Creates a blank, snazzy-looking newsletter
Pleading	Creates a pleading, a legal document
Resume	Helps you whip up a spiffy-looking resume
Table	Builds and formats a table

WordBasic WordBasic is Word's built-in programming language. WordBasic is way cool. It's also way, way beyond the scope of this little book. For information about WordBasic, see your Word user documentation.

 Macro

Word Count

You can easily count the number of pages, words, characters, paragraphs, and lines in a document. To do so, first be sure the document is active and then choose the Tools Word Count command. Word displays the Word Count dialog box, and after a few milliseconds of counting, it shows the document statistics.

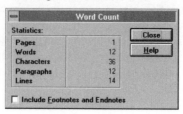

WordPerfect

WordPerfect is another very popular word-processor application. Because many, many people use WordPerfect, you should know that it's possible to move, or export, Word documents to WordPerfect and move, or import, WordPerfect documents into Word.

Moving a Document from Word to WordPerfect

Choose the File Save As command. Complete the dialog box in the usual way except specify the file type as the appropriate WordPerfect file. To do this, activate the Save File As Type list box and choose a list entry.

Moving a Document from WordPerfect to Word

Save the Document in WordPerfect. Then start Word and choose the File Open command. Complete the dialog box in the usual way except specify the file type as the saved-in WordPerfect file format. To do this, activate the List Files of Type list box and choose a list entry.

Exporting Documents; Importing Documents

Word Wrap

Word wrap just means that Word moves the **insertion point** to the next line once you run out of room on the current line. Because it wants to be helpful, Word will also move big words to the next line if the move makes things fit better. Word wrap is a simple little feature, but it's one of the big reasons that word-processors such as Word are much, much easier to use than typewriters.

 **Nonbreaking Spaces**

Zooming

You can magnify and reduce, or shrink, the size of the characters shown on your screen. You can use either the View Zoom command or the Standard toolbar's Zoom Control drop-down list box.

Magnifying

Activate the Zoom Control drop-down box on the Standard toolbar or choose the View Zoom command. Then select a percentage. Selecting 200%, for example, magnifies everything to twice its actual size.

Shrinking

Activate the Zoom drop-down list box on the Standard toolbar or choose the View Zoom command. Then select a percentage. Selecting 50%, for example, reduces everything to half its actual size.

 **Actual size may vary**

When you zoom a document, you don't change the character point size. You merely magnify or shrink the display. As a result, zooming doesn't change what your printed document looks like. To do that, you use the Format Font command.

TROUBLE-SHOOTING

Got a problem? Starting on the next page are solutions to the problems that plague new users of Microsoft Word. You'll be on your way—and safely out of danger—in no time.

TABLES

You Can't Get Table Gridlines to Print

Word displays table gridlines to make it easier for you to see a table's columns and rows. The gridlines, therefore, are for display purposes only. They don't print. If you want to print lines to show a table's rows and columns, you'll need to add borders.

If table gridlines don't show

You can turn on and off the display of table gridlines by choosing the Table Gridlines command. When the display is turned on, Word places a check mark in front of the command name.

AutoFormat a table

The easiest way to add border lines to a table is by choosing the Table Table AutoFormat command. Follow these steps:

1 Select the table.

2 Choose the Table Table AutoFormat command.

3 When Word displays the Table AutoFormat dialog box, select a table from the list.

Add a border grid

Another way to add border lines to a table is by choosing the Format Borders and Shading command. To do this, follow these steps:

1 Select the table.

2 Choose the Format Borders and Shading command.

3 Mark the Borders tab.

4 Select the Presets Grid button.

Borders; Paragraphs

You Can't Get a Table Formula to Calculate

The formulas you enter into table cells aren't updated automatically. You need to tell Word when it's time to recalculate.

Manually force recalculation

To tell Word it should recalculate a formula, click the formula and press F9.

You Can't Correctly Calculate a Table Formula

If you're just starting out, this can be mighty frustrating. But, rest assured, Word is calculating the formula correctly. The problem, as painful as it may be to admit, is that the formula you've entered isn't actually the one you want to calculate. In a nutshell, your problem probably boils down to one of operator precedence.

Override the standard operator precedence

To force Word to calculate in the order you want, enclose the calculation you want made first in parentheses. Then enclose the calculation you want made second in parentheses. Then enclose the calculation you want made third in parentheses, and so on.

Formulas

PRINTING

You Want to Stop Page Breaking

Sometimes Word will break a document across pages—even though you don't want it. As a practical matter, you can't actually tell Word not to page break. It page breaks because it's run out of room on a page. You can change where Word page breaks, however, by increasing the page space available for printing and by condensing page information.

continues

You Want to Stop Page Breaking *(continued)*

Change the page dimensions

One of the easier ways you can stop or minimize a document's page breaking is to reduce the margins. Reducing the left and right margins makes lines longer, of course. And reducing the top and bottom margins lets you add lines to pages. Smaller page margins, therefore, increase the printable page area.

To reduce the page margins, choose the File Page Setup command, select the Margins tab, and then change the margin settings.

Reduce the font size

Another way to pack more information onto a page and thereby potentially stop page breaking—or at least reduce it—is to use a smaller point size. You can do this by entering a smaller number in the font size box.

Another approach is to use a narrower font—such as a condensed font. You can do this by selecting another, proportional, more tightly packed font from the font box.

Previewing pages

Remember, to see what your printed pages will look like, choose the View Page Layout command or the Page Layout view button.

You Want to Cancel a Printing Document

If you've told Word to print a document you later realize you don't want to print, you may want to cancel the printing. This is particularly true if the document is long and you'd really prefer not to waste the paper.

Press Esc if you're foreground printing

If Word shows a message box on your screen that says something along the lines of "Printing Document," you can cancel the printing by pressing Esc or by clicking the message box's Cancel command button.

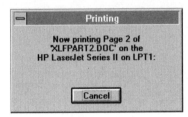

Double-click the printer picture if you're background printing

If Word is background printing, the status bar shows a picture of a little printer spewing out sheets of paper. If you double-click this printer picture, Word stops background printing.

continues

You Want to Cancel a Printing Document *(continued)*

Switch to the Print Manager and delete the job

When Word prints a document either in the background or in the foreground, it creates a print spool file that it sends to the Windows Print Manager. The Print Manager then prints this print spool file as well as any other print spool files Word and other applications have sent.

To cancel a printing Word document once it's been sent to the Print Manager, you need to follow these steps:

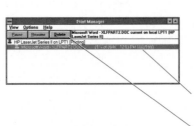

1 Choose the Word Control menu's Switch To command—for example, by pressing Ctrl+Esc.

2 Select the Print Manager application from the Task List—for example, by double-clicking.

3 Click the printing Word document.

4 Select the Print Manager's Delete command button.

🐾 **Control-menu Commands; Printing; Switching Tasks**

DISPLAY

You Can't See the Menu

If you choose the View Full Screen command, Word shows only the document on the screen. It doesn't show the application window title bar, the menu bar, or the toolbars. If you aren't familiar with the full screen view, it can be a bit confusing.

Click the full screen button

If you or someone else has just switched to the full screen view, Word displays a full screen button. Click it to return to the regular, normal screen view.

Choose the View Normal command

If someone has removed the full screen button by double-clicking its Control menu box, you obviously can't use it to return to the normal view. You can, however, choose the View Normal command. To do this, press Alt+V to activate the View menu. Then press N to choose the Normal command. In other words, you can still activate the same old menus with the Alt key—you just need to remember which letters activate which menus since they aren't displayed.

If you need to know the menu and command hotkeys

If you do start working with the full screen view and need to know which letters, or hotkeys, you press with Alt to activate menus, check the Quick Reference section of this book. It lists all the commands and their corresponding hotkeys.

You Can't See Graphics on the Screen

If you don't see the graphic images or drawn objects you've added, your problem may be solved in any of three ways.

Turn Off Draft Output

If you (or someone else) turned on Word's Draft Output option, Word displays a document without formatting or graphics. To turn off the Draft Output option, follow these steps:

1 Choose the Tools Options command.

2 Select the Print tab.

3 Unmark the Draft Output check box—for example, by clicking it.

continues

You Can't See Graphics on the Screen *(continued)*

Turn On Drawing Objects

If it's just drawn objects that aren't showing up, it may also be that someone—nobody will say who—turned off Word's Drawing Objects. To get this ball rolling again, follow these steps:

1 Choose the Tools Options command.

2 Select the Print tab.

3 Mark the Drawing Objects check box if it isn't already marked.

Free memory

One other potential problem is this: Word may not have enough memory to draw and display fancy schmancy things like drawn objects. You can address this problem by closing inactive Word **documents**.

Another thing you can do is switch to any of your other open applications and close them. You can switch to the other open applications by choosing the Word Control menu's Switch To command, selecting the other application from the Task List dialog box, and then choosing the other application's File Exit command.

 Control-menu Commands; Switching Tasks

FILES

You Can't Save
a Document

Word needs a certain amount of system horsepower—principally memory—to save a document. If your system resources get too low, therefore, you can run into some pretty serious problems. Fortunately, as long as you keep your cool, this doesn't have to be a disaster. Your basic tack is a simple one. You want to free up system resources and then try resaving the document.

Close your other open applications

Switch to any of your other open applications and close them. You can switch to the other open applications by choosing the Word Control menu's Switch To command, selecting the other application from the Task List dialog box, and then choosing the other application's File Exit command.

Once you've closed all the other applications (and saved their documents if that's appropriate), return to Word and try resaving the document you couldn't earlier save.

If you're the superstitious sort, go ahead and cross your fingers. It won't make any difference. But it may make you feel better.

Try opening another session of Word or Write

If you've closed all the other open Windows applications and still can't save the document, you can try starting Windows Write or another copy of Word and then using that application to save the document. This may work because in some cases even though you've freed up system resources Word can't use those resources. (Weird, huh?) A newly started application, however, may be able to use the resources. So here's what you can do:

1 Start Write or a second copy of Word. (Refer to the Word A to Z entry **Switching Tasks** if this isn't something you know how to do right off the top of your head.)

2 Copy the unsavable document to the Clipboard by selecting it and choosing Edit Copy.

3 Switch to the newly started application—for example, by pressing Ctrl+Esc and double-clicking the application on the Task List dialog box.

4 Paste the Clipboard contents into the new document by choosing Edit Paste.

5 Save the new document using a new file name.

 Saving Documents

You Can't Find a Document

Sure, this is a bummer. But a lost document doesn't have to be as big a problem as you think.

Use the File Find File command

You can usually use the File Find File command to locate documents. When you choose the command, Word displays the Find File dialog box.

On the left half of the dialog box, Word lists all document files on your disk. You can scroll through the list to find the document file you want.

Word shows a picture of the selected document if the View drop-down list shows Preview.

You can choose other Views too. The File Info view shows MS-DOS file information. The Summary view shows the information you enter into the File Summary dialog box, which Word displays the first time you save a document.

When you find the document you want, select Open.

The first time you use File Find File

The first time—and only the first time—you (or someone else) uses the File Find File command, Word displays the Search dialog box. This dialog box lets you describe the criteria you want to use to search for document files, the disk you want to search, and the directories you want to search.

You Accidentally Erased a Document

If you've just erased a document you now realize you desperately need, stop what you're doing. Don't save anything else to your hard disk. It may be possible to recover, or unerase, a document file.

Use the MS-DOS Undelete command

How you unerase document files is beyond the scope of this little book: The mechanics relate to MS-DOS and not to Word. So you'll need to look up the File Undelete command in your MS-DOS user documentation.

I will say this. When MS-DOS deletes a file, it doesn't actually erase the document disk file. Instead, it simply adds the document's disk space to its list of locations that can now be used to store new data. Eventually, the document file data will be overwritten with some new file. But, if you haven't yet saved a new file over the old document's disk location, the document still exists. In this case, you can undelete the file.

 Opening Documents; Saving Documents

You Can't Remember Your Password

If you or someone else assigned a read reservation password to a document file using the Save Options command button, you'll need to supply that password from now on before you open the file. If you forget your password or can't seem to enter it correctly, Word won't let you open the document.

Try a password with different-case letters

Word differentiates passwords on the basis of the letter case. The following words, for example, are all different passwords from Word's point-of-view: Wathers, wATHERS, and WATHERS. For this reason, if you think you know the password, try changing all the lowercase letters to uppercase letters and vice versa. It may be that you entered the password with a different combination of upper- and lowercase letters than you think. (This can occur, for instance, if you happened to press the Caps Lock key before entering the password.)

 Opening Documents; Save Options; Saving Documents

WINDOWS AND APPLICATIONS

You've Started More Than One Copy of Word

If you begin multitasking with the Control menu's Switch To command, it's not all that difficult to find you've started multiple copies of Word. This consumes system resources—such as memory. And it makes it difficult to share data across documents.

Exit from the active Word application

If one of the Word applications is active—meaning the Word application window shows on your screen—you can exit from it. (Do this with the File Exit command.) This closes the active Word task, but the other inactive Word task will still be open, or running.

Close the second Word task

If another application or the Program Manager is active, follow these steps to close the second, extra Word task:

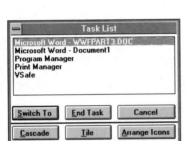

1 Choose the application Control menu's Switch To command—for example, by pressing Ctrl+Esc.

2 Select one of the Word applications from the task list—for example, by double-clicking.

3 When the Word application window appears, choose the File Exit command.

Control-menu Commands; Switching Tasks

You Can't Get an Application— such as Word— to Respond

It's unlikely but still possible that a bug in Word or a bug in some other program will cause an application to stop responding. If this happens, you won't be able to choose menu commands. And you may not be able to move the mouse pointer.

Terminate the unresponsive application

Unfortunately, if an application truly is unresponsive, if it ignores your keyboard and mouse actions, there's nothing you can do to make it start responding again. When this is the case, however, you can press Ctrl+Alt+Delete.

Ctrl+Alt+Delete—you press the 3 keys simultaneously—tells Windows to look at the active application and check for responsiveness. Windows makes this check and displays a message that tells you whether the application is, in fact, unresponsive.

continues

You Can't Get an Application to Respond *(continued)*

```
This Windows application has stopped responding to the system.

* Press ESC to cancel and return to Windows.
* Press ENTER to close this application that is not responding.
  You will lose any unsaved information in this application.
* Press CTRL+ALT+DELETE to restart your computer. You will
  lose any unsaved information in all applications.

        Press ENTER for OK or ESC to cancel: OK
```

As the message text indicates, you can simply press Enter to close the unresponsive application. By the way, if the application isn't unresponsive, Windows knows this, and the message text indicates as much. In this case, you can press Enter to return to the application.

Patience is a virtue

Before you conclude that Word or some other application is ignoring you, consider the possibility that it is busy instead. Word, for example, may be running a macro or a WordBasic module. Other applications may be printing to a spool file (which gets sent to the Print Manager for printing) or may be executing some command you've given.

You Get an Application Error

Sometimes an application asks Windows to do the impossible. When this happens—which isn't very often since the advent of Windows version 3.1, thankfully—Windows displays a message box that says there's been an application error.

Close the application

When Windows does alert you to an application error, it usually gives you two choices. You can close the application, or you can ignore the error.

QUICK REFERENCE

Any time you explore some exotic location, you're bound to see flora and fauna you can't identify. To make sure you can identify the commands and toolbar buttons you see in Microsoft Word, the Quick Reference describes these items in systematic detail.

File Menu

New	Opens a new, blank document based on the document template you select
Open...	Retrieves an existing document
Close	Removes the active document's window from the screen
Save	Resaves the active document as long as you've already saved it once before
Save As...	Saves a document the first time
Save All	Resaves all the active documents
Find File...	Looks for documents matching a specified description
Summary Info...	Displays information about the active document
Templates...	Changes the template attached to the document
Page Setup...	Describes the layout of printed document pages
Print Preview	Displays a window showing how printed document pages will look
Print...	Prints the active document
Exit	Closes, or stops, the Microsoft Word application

Numbered File menu commands

Word also lists as File menu commands the last four documents you saved. You can open a listed document by selecting it from the File menu.

Edit Menu

Undo	Reverses, or undoes, the last document change
Repeat	Duplicates the last document change
Cut	Moves the current document selection to the Clipboard
Copy	Moves a copy of the current document selection to the Clipboard
Paste	Moves the Clipboard contents to the active document
Paste Special...	Moves some portion of the Clipboard contents to the active document
Clear	Erases the current selection
Select All	Selects the entire document
Find...	Looks for text or formatting matching a specified description
Replace...	Looks for text or formatting matching specified description and, optionally, replaces it
Go To...	Moves the insertion point
AutoText...	Lets you create and enter autotext entries
Bookmark...	Lets you create and move the insertion point to bookmarks
Links...	Describes, updates, and changes selected object's link
Object	Opens selected object so that it can be modified

View Menu

Normal	Displays document as a single column of text
Outline	Displays an outline of document's headings
Page Layout	Displays document as laid-out pages
Master Document	Switches to the master document view
F**u**ll Screen	Displays only the document on the screen
Toolbars...	Lets you specify which toolbars should appear on your screen
Ruler	Turns off and on the ruler display
Header and Footer	Opens header and footer editing area on laid-out pages
Footnotes	Opens the footnote pane at the bottom of the document window
Annotations	Opens the annotations pane at the bottom of the document window
Zoom...	Magnifies and reduces the on-screen document by a set percentage

Insert Menu

Break...	Breaks column, page, or section at the insertion point
Page N**u**mbers...	Numbers pages of document
Annotation	Places a note at the insertion point and opens annotation pane
Date and **T**ime...	Places the current date or time at the insertion point
Fi**e**ld...	Places a field code at the insertion point
Symbol...	Adds a symbol to the document at the insertion point

For<u>m</u> Field...	Places a new form field at the insertion point
Foot<u>n</u>ote...	Places a footnote or endnote at the insertion point and opens footnote or endnote pane
Capt<u>i</u>on...	Places a figure caption above or below the selected object
Cross-<u>r</u>eference...	Adds a cross-reference entry for selected term
Inde<u>x</u> and Tables...	Adds an index, table of contents, table of figures, or table of authorities
Fi<u>l</u>e...	Inserts another document file's contents into the open document at the insertion point
<u>F</u>rame	Inserts an empty frame or adds a frame to selected object
<u>P</u>icture...	Adds a picture from a graphic image file to the document
<u>O</u>bject...	Embeds or links another application's object to the document
<u>D</u>atabase...	Adds records from an external database to the document

F<u>o</u>rmat Menu

<u>F</u>ont...	Changes font and spacing of selected characters
<u>P</u>aragraph...	Changes indenting, alignment, and numbering of selected paragraph
<u>T</u>abs...	Sets and clears tab stops for selected paragraphs
<u>B</u>orders and Shading...	Changes borders and shading of selected paragraphs, tables, and pictures
<u>C</u>olumns...	Changes the number of columns used in a document section
Change Ca<u>s</u>e...	Changes case of the selected letters
<u>D</u>rop Cap...	Lets you create dropped capital letters. Very cool.

continues

Format Menu *(continued)*

Bullets and <u>N</u>umbering...	Adds bullets or numbers to selected paragraphs
<u>H</u>eading Numbering...	Adds numbers to selected headings
<u>A</u>utoFormat...	Formats the current document selection so that it looks pretty
Style <u>G</u>allery...	Shows how document looks with different styles
<u>S</u>tyle...	Lets you apply and create styles
Fra<u>m</u>e...	Changes how text flows around a framed object
Pictu<u>r</u>e...	Crops and scales selected picture
Drawing <u>O</u>bject...	Changes colors and line thickness of drawn objects

<u>T</u>ools Menu

<u>S</u>pelling...	Checks spelling of current document selection
<u>G</u>rammar...	Checks grammar of current document selection
<u>T</u>hesaurus...	Shows synonyms and antonyms for selected word
<u>H</u>yphenation...	Lets you specify how Word should hyphenate words
<u>L</u>anguage...	Specifies which language dictionary should be used for checking spelling and other proofing
<u>W</u>ord Count...	Counts the pages, words, characters, paragraphs, lines in document
<u>A</u>utoCorrect...	Determines which automatic typing corrections Word should make
Mail Me<u>r</u>ge...	Generates form letters, labels, envelopes, and catalogs

Envelopes and Labels...	Prints envelopes and labels
Protect Document...	Protects a document by limiting changes
Re**v**isions...	Tells Word to mark document changes with revision marks
Macro...	Records, runs, creates, or deletes Word Basic macros
Customize...	Customizes Word's toolbars, menus, and shortcut keys
Options...	Controls Word's operation with a 12-page dialog box packed with a rich, eclectic set of options

T**a**ble Menu

Insert...	Adds cells, columns, rows to a table
Delete...	Removes cells, columns, rows from a table
Merge...	Combines selected cells
S**p**lit...	Splits previously merged cells
Select **R**ow	Selects the row with the selected cell
Select **C**olumn	Selects the column with the selected cell
Select T**a**ble	Selects the table with the selected cell
Table Auto**F**ormat...	Formats the selected table so that it looks nice
Cell Height and **W**idth...	Lets you adjust selected cell's column widths and row heights
Headings...	Tells Word to print table heading rows at the start of page on which the table appears
Con**v**ert Table to Text...	Lets you turn tables into regular text and regular text into tables
Sort...	Arranges the selected table rows or the selected paragraphs

continues

Table Menu *(continued)*

F̲ormula...	Adds a formula to the selected cell
S̲plit Table...	Splits a table above the selected row by inserting paragraph
Gridl̲ines...	Turns on and off the display of table gridlines

Changing command names

The Convert Table to Text and Sort commands work on both text and table rows. Therefore, the command name changes to reflect the current document selection.

W̲indow Menu

N̲ew Window	Opens a new window onto the active document
A̲rrange All	Displays all open document windows in tiles
Sp̲lit/Remove Sp̲lit	Splits/unsplits the active document window

Your commands are numbered

Word also lists all the open document windows as numbered Window menu commands. You can activate a listed window by choosing it from the Window menu.

H̲elp Menu

C̲ontents	Lists the major help topic categories
S̲earch for Help on...	Provides help on a topic you specify
I̲ndex...	Lists all the individual help topics
Q̲uick Preview...	Starts the online tutorial about Word for Windows
E̲xamples and Demos...	Starts the online tutorial, Learning Microsoft Word
Ti̲p of the Day...	Displays a Word tip in a message box

WordPerfect Help...	Tells the Word way to accomplish a WordPerfect task
Technical Support...	Tells about support available for Microsoft Word
About Microsoft Word...	Displays the copyright notice, the software version number, and system information about your computer

Standard Toolbar Tools

	Opens a new, blank document
	Displays the Open dialog box so that you can retrieve an existing document
	Saves the active document on disk
	Prints the active document
	Shows what the printed pages of a document will look like
	Checks the spelling of words in the active document
	Moves the current document selection to the Clipboard
	Moves a copy of the current document selection to the Clipboard
	Moves the Clipboard contents to the active document
	Copies formatting of current document selection to the next document selection
	Undoes the last document change
	Redoes the last action that was undone
	Automatically formats current document selection
	Inserts an AutoText entry

continues

Standard Toolbar Tools *(continued)*

Inserts a table
Inserts a Microsoft Excel worksheet
Changes the number of text columns per page
Starts the Drawing tool so that you can add a drawn object to document
Starts Microsoft Graph so that you can add a chart to document
Shows and hides nonprinting characters
100% Magnifies or reduces document contents by specified zoom percentage
Displays help information about whatever you next click: a command, a piece of a document, or some element of the application or document window Very handy.

Formatting Toolbar Tools

Normal Changes style of document selection
Times New Roman Changes font of document selection
10 Changes font/point size of document selection
B Bolds characters in document selection
I Italicizes characters in document selection
U Underlines characters in document selection
Left-aligns selected paragraphs
Centers selected paragraphs
Right-aligns selected paragraphs

	Justifies selected paragraphs
	Numbers selected paragraphs
	Adds bullets to each of selected paragraphs
	Decreases the indenting of selected paragraphs
	Increases the indenting of selected paragraphs
	Displays the Borders toolbar

Drawing Toolbar Tools

	Draws a straight line
	Draws rectangles and squares
	Draws ellipses and circles
	Draws arcs
	Draws freeform shapes
	Adds a text box
	Adds a callout
	Changes format of a callout
	Colors interior of drawn objects
	Colors the border line of drawn objects
	Changes the line style and thickness
	Selects multiple objects you want to group
	Restacks objects so that selected object is at bottom of the pile
	Restacks objects so that the selected object is at the top of the pile
	Moves selected object so that it's in front of text

continues

Drawing Toolbar Tools *(continued)*

	Moves selected object so that it's behind text
	Groups selected objects
	Ungroups a previously grouped set of objects
	Flips selected object horizontally
	Flips selected object vertically
	Rotates the selected object 90 degrees
	Adds selection handles to selected object so that it can be resized
	Adds a grid of horizontal and vertical lines for alignment and positioning
	Vertically or horizontally aligns the selected object
	Creates a picture by drawing
	Inserts a frame for selected object

C

Q

R

S

X

Z

The manuscript for this book was prepared and submitted to Microsoft Press in electronic form. Text files were prepared using Microsoft Word 2.0 for Windows. Pages were composed by Stephen L. Nelson, Inc. using PageMaker 5.0 for Windows, with text in Minion and display type in Copperplate. Composed pages were delivered to the printer as electronic prepress files.

COVER DESIGNER
Rebecca Geisler

COVER ILLUSTRATOR
Eldon Doty

COVER COLOR SEPARATOR
Color Service, Inc.

INTERIOR TEXT DESIGNER
The Understanding Business

PAGE LAYOUT AND TYPOGRAPHY
Greg Schultz and Stefan Knorr

EDITOR
Pat Coleman

TECHNICAL EDITOR
Clay Martin

INDEXER
Julie Kawabata

Printed on recycled paper stock.

This book was not tested on animals.

Train Yourself
with *Step by Step* books from Microsoft Press

The *Step by Step* books are the perfect self-paced training solution for the businessperson. Whether you are a new user or are upgrading from a previous version of the software, the *Step by Step* books can teach you exactly what you need to know to get the most from your new software. Each lesson is modular, example-rich, and fully integrated with a timesaving practice file on the disk. So if you're too busy to attend class, or if classroom training doesn't make sense for you or your office, you can build the computer skills you need with the *Step by Step* books from Microsoft Press.

Microsoft® Word 6 for Windows™ Step by Step
Catapult, Inc.
336 pages, softcover with one 3.5-inch disk
$29.95 ($39.95 Canada)   ISBN 1-55615-576-X

Microsoft® Excel 5 for Windows™ Step by Step
Catapult, Inc.
368 pages, softcover with one 3.5-inch disk
$29.95 ($39.95 Canada)   ISBN 1-55615-587-5

*Microsoft*Press

More Step by Step *Books*
from Microsoft Press

Microsoft® Excel Visual Basic® for Applications Step by Step
Reed Jacobson

Covers Microsoft Excel version 5 for Windows.
350 pages, softcover with one 3.5-inch disk
$29.95 ($39.95 Canada)   ISBN 1-55615-589-1

Microsoft® Windows™ 3.1 Step by Step
Catapult, Inc.

296 pages, softcover with one 3.5-inch disk
$29.95 ($39.95 Canada)   ISBN 1-55615-501-8

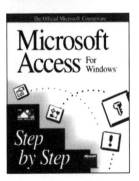

Microsoft Access® for Windows™ Step by Step
Microsoft Corporation

Covers version 1.0.
384 pages, softcover with one 3.5-inch disk
$29.95 ($39.95 Canada)   ISBN 1-55615-482-8
Updated edition available March 1994

MicrosoftPress

Get Quick Answers
with the Microsoft® Field Guides

Field Guide to Microsoft® Excel 5 for Windows™
Stephen L. Nelson
208 pages, softcover   4³/₄ x 8 $9.95 ($12.95 Canada)
ISBN 1-55615-579-4

Field Guide to MS-DOS®
Versions 6.0 and 6.2
Siechert & Wood
208 pages, softcover   4³/₄ x 8 $9.95 ($12.95 Canada)
ISBN 1-55615-560-3

Field Guide to Microsoft® Windows™ 3.1
Stephen L. Nelson
208 pages, softcover   4³/₄ x 8 $9.95 ($12.95 Canada)
ISBN 1-55615-640-5
Available March 1994

MicrosoftPress